Generis

PUBLISHING

Computer Languages and Digitalization

Dušan Tošić

Title: **Computer Languages and Digitalization**

ISBN: 979-8-89966-472-4

Author: Dušan Tošić

Cover image: www.pixabay.com

Publisher: Generis Publishing
Online orders: www.generis-publishing.com
Contact email: info@generis-publishing.com

Dušan Tošić

Computer languages and digitalization

2026

CONTENTS

PREFACE

The main part of this book consists of a collection of works that the author has published (in some works as a co-author) over the past twenty years. Despite the fact that the book is composed of different works, it represents a whole because all the works are related to computer languages and digitalization. At the same time, the works are not arranged chronologically as they were created, but logically so that the previous works contribute to a better understanding of the following ones. In addition, almost every work has been slightly modified so that it fits as well as possible into the whole.

I owe a great deal of gratitude to Olga Pomogaibog, who suggested that I write this book and always encouraged me to finish writing as soon as possible.

1.
INTRODUCTION

1.1. Digitalization and languages

Modern computers operate with various types of languages, starting from machine language (a language created over the binary alphabet, i.e. over the symbols 0 and 1) and up to natural (spoken) languages which, primarily, serve for communication between people. Language is used to present and transmit information. Information can be represented as analog or digital. The digital information is "discrete and pure" while analog information is "continuous and noisy". Digital technology is based on operating with digital data, while analog technology is based on operating with analog data.

The process in which analog symbols are replaced by digits (represented by digits) is called **digitization**, and if, in addition, the translated data is operated with an impact on the environment, it is **digitalization**. These terms are often confused, so we will further define their meaning and role more precisely.

Any operation to be realized on modern computers, its realization comes down to digitization, i.e. operating with digits 0 and 1. Conversely, digitization would not have the role it has today if it was not so tightly connected with electronic computers. This means that without digitization, modern computers, such as we use today, would not exist. So, digitalization was started with the appearance of the first electronic calculators (although some would say even earlier with the appearance of Booll's algebra).

From the first uses to the present, the concept of discretization has evolved and today digitalization is present in almost all human activities. Practically, wherever electronic computers are used, digitization is present.

How did the inextricable link between digital computers and digitization come about? In the thirties of the twentieth century, there was extensive experimentation with both digital and analog computers. During that period, it is not clear which type of computer should be preferred. However, when the first digital electronic computer (ENIAC, 1946) worked, it was clear in which direction the development of computers would move because digital technology completely supplanted analog. In work [1], the entire history of computers is divided into 2 periods: pre-electronic and electronic. At the end of the pre-electronic period, analog and digital computers were developed in parallel, but digital computers soon won the primacy. In the beginning, digitization was limited to expressing quantities in binary digits and operating with them. Between the 40s and 60s of the 20th century, digitalization completely displaced analog technology. It has become present in all areas where computers are used. This process is known as the "digital revolution" [3]. The digital revolution has contributed to the digitization of almost all aspects of society - especially the economy. In the document [4] it is written: "Since the late 1980s, the digital revolution has transformed the economy and society. First came the development of a connected economy, characterized by mass take-up of the Internet and the roll-out of broadband networks. This was followed by the development of a digital economy via the increasing use of digital platforms as business models for the supply of goods and services. Now the movement is towards a digitalized economy whose production and consumption models are based on the incorporation of digital technologies in all economic, social and environmental dimensions."

In [2] the terms digitization, digitalization and digital transformation are defined as follows:

Digitization is the process of converting analog information into digital information. This includes the transfer of data to digital media such as computers, tablets and smartphones.

Digitalization is the process of using digital data obtained from analog data through digitization and new technologies to create new digital ecosystems, automated processes and greater efficiency in the processing, storage and transmission of this data.

Digital transformation describes the process of switching from traditional business models and working methods to digital technologies and processes."

Digitalization itself can also be defined as the integration of digital technologies and digitized data across the economy and society. Digitalization has changed and improved many human activities in recent years. Thanks to digitization, significant progress has been achieved in: Manufacturing industry, Financial world, Healthcare, Education, etc. All types of binis experienced a special boom.

1.2. Programming languages, classification and digitalization

Language is a set of rules for communication between two or more subjects. Language is used to present and transmit information. All languages can be classified into two categories: natural and artificial. Natural languages are used for communication between people in spoken or written form. Artificial languages are created for use in certain areas where the use of natural languages is not suitable. Artificial languages include programming languages. Computer languages are artificial languages and are somehow related to computers. Programming languages serve primarily for communication between humans and computers (sometimes it is also used for communication between people!) There is no strict (mathematical) definition of a programming language. However, there are various descriptive definitions. Thus, we can define a programming language as a set of syntactic and semantic rules used for the description (definition) of computer programs. Until now, a large number of computer languages have been created, many of which are "dead languages", i.e. they are no longer used. What impact does digitalization have on languages, in general, and especially on programming languages? With the appearance of the first digital computers, the so-called "machine languages" created over the binary alphabet, ie. digits 0 and 1. So, digit was basic term for programming language and from this concept are derived concepts digization and digitalization. Why was the binary alphabet used? In nature, there are often 2 stable states (voltage - no voltage, north magnetic pole - south magnetic pole, current flows - does not flow current,...) so it is convenient to mark these states with numbers 0 and 1. It was easy to operate with them using computer hardware. In this way, the digitization essential for digital computers was carried out. The role of digitization was essential, although it was not emphasized at the time. The impact of digitization depended on the type of language. In this period, programming languages played a dominant role. As the number of programming languages grew rapidly, the need for their classification arose.

1.2.1 Programming Language classifications

There are various classifications of programming languages depending on the chosen classification criteria [8]. However, none of them is strict enough; each classification, given here, should be accepted conditionally. In practice, it often happens that programming languages have characteristics of different classes, so it is difficult to classify them into just one class.

1.2.2. Classification according to the degree of computer dependency

This is one of the most general classifications because it includes all programming languages [8]. According to the degree of computer dependency, all programming languages are divided into:

- machine-dependent languages and
- machine-independent languages.

Machine-dependent languages are divided into:

- machine languages
- machine-oriented languages.

Machine-oriented languages are divided into:

- symbolic languages and
- macro languages.

Machine-independent languages are divided into:

- procedural-oriented languages and
- problem-oriented languages.

Machine-independent languages are often called high-level programming languages. When studying programming languages, this class is the most interesting.

Let us briefly describe the characteristics of each of the mentioned classes of programming languages.

The most elementary programming language is the internal language of the computer (machine), the so-called machine language. As already mentioned, machine language is built on the binary alphabet, i.e. all information in the machine language of today's computers is represented using the symbols 0 and 1. The hardware of modern computers has led to everything in machine language being expressed using these two symbols.

A cell is a physical object in a computer that can store a single bit (bit), i.e. a binary 0 or 1. Cells are organized into fixed-length arrays, and these arrays form the computer's memory. An organized array of fixed-length cells, which has its own address, is called a memory location. Since the contents of the cells are variable, different variations composed of zeros and ones can be represented in one memory location. One such variation determines a binary word, the length of which is equal to the number of cells in the memory location. A binary word of length 8 is called a byte. In most modern computers, the smallest addressable memory location is 8 cells long, the name of which is regularly identified with the name of a binary word of length 8, so memory capacity is regularly expressed in bytes. In addition to the byte, the most commonly used lengths of memory locations are 2 bytes (word), 4 bytes (double word), 8 bytes, etc.

An algorithm is written in machine language in a series of memory locations. Data and operations are encoded with zeros and ones, so that the algorithm is represented in a unique way in the computer [7].

The basic component of machine language is the instruction. An instruction usually consists of an operation code and the addresses of the operands.

Let two memory locations be labeled a and b and their addresses be, respectively: 00111101 and 00011111. If the addition operation code is: 11011011, then the instruction to add the contents of memory locations a and b, in machine language, has the form:

11011011 00111101 00011111

A sequence of instructions of this type forms a machine language program.

Machine languages for different types of computers are different and it doesn't make much sense to program in machine language.

Symbolic (assembly) languages were developed from machine language by replacing the operation code with a mnemonic abbreviation - mnemonic code - and the operand addresses with symbolic addresses. Operation codes and operand addresses are represented by alphabetic or numeric characters. Each instruction in symbolic language corresponds to only one machine language instruction.

For example, the machine language instruction:

110110110011110100011111

could be written in symbolic language as follows:

ADD a, b

where:

• ADD is the mnemonic for the addition operation and replaces the code 11011011,

• a is the symbolic address of the first operand and replaces the address 00111101,

• b is the symbolic address of the second operand and replaces the address 00011111.

An algorithm written in symbolic language cannot be executed on a computer, but must be translated into machine language. The language processor for symbolic language is called an assembler, which is why symbolic languages are often called assembly languages. Assemblers are the simplest language processors due to the unambiguous correspondence of mnemonics and symbolic addresses with codes and machine addresses.

Programming in symbolic language makes sense because in this way the computer resources can be best used and the best program performance can be achieved. However, in order to successfully program in symbolic language, it is necessary to know the technical characteristics of the computer, and the programming process itself remains a laborious task.

Macro-languages were created from symbolic languages by adding macro-commands. One macro-command corresponds to a group of instructions in symbolic language. In this way, macro-language approaches human spoken language and programming becomes easier.

For example, instead of a series of instructions for loading an integer in symbolic language, in macro-language one can write:

READ a.

This loads an integer from the input device and stores it at symbolic address a. Anywhere in the program where an integer needs to be loaded, the previous command can be used, of course with the corresponding symbolic address specified.

Macro-instructions are interconnected by symbolic instructions, and in this way a program in a macro-language is formed. Therefore, a macro-language is difficult to separate from a symbolic one, i.e. a large number of features of a symbolic language can also be attributed to a macro-language.

Macro language compilers are called macro-assemblers and are most often in the same package with an assembler. In most assembly languages, there is a possibility for the user to create their own macro-instructions, i.e. their own macro-language.

Symbolic macro-languages can in most cases be successfully replaced by the high-level programming language **C**, which is much more convenient for programming. Therefore, an increasing number of programmers use symbolic and macro- languages.

The researchers paid the main attention to creating a programming language that would be as similar as possible to human spoken language with the possibility of using it on various types of computers (practically, on computers from different manufacturers).

By doing so, they contributed to rapid digitization. We can say that such a language is machine independent (it does not depend on the type of computer), and for some programs that they are portable from one computer to another, without changes. The first language created in this way was the programming language FORTRAN Despite the fact that these are said to be machine-independent languages, complete independence from the type of computer is almost never achieved. The user must always keep in mind the specifics of the implementation of the programming language on a specific type of computer. This is the problem of portabilityand it is (somewhat) solved by the standardization of the language. Namely, for a language was required to have a core that would be common to all types of computers. If anyone wanted to make a portable program, they only had to use the capabilities (ie commands) of the kernel. The powerful computer manufacturers did not always adhere to the writing of portable programs, but tried to impose their own rules. After the creation of FORTRAN, a series of machine-independent languages (so-called high languages) appeared, with an effort to create a language that would be most suitable for humans. In order for a programming language to be acceptable to a larger number of programmers, it should have a number of positive characteristics ([5], [6]), such as:

- simplicity
- uniformity
- ability to describe and use abstractions
- expressiveness
- portability
- easy translation
- modularity
- orthogonality
- ....

Additionally, a programming language should generate efficient, safe, and human-readable programs. In an effort to create a language that would satisfy as many desirable features as possible (some of which are contradictory, for example simplicity and expressiveness), hundreds of programming languages have been created. Most procedural languages are designed to solve a wide range of problems, i.e. most of them claim to be universal. Despite this, many have turned out to be suitable for solving problems of certain narrower classes.

Digitalization has led to the emergence of a category of computer users that is becoming larger and more significant every day. These are people with different profiles who use computers to solve more or less stereotypical tasks, but are not familiar with programming and the use of procedural languages. This category includes scientists from various fields, administrative, accounting, banking, tourism and other officials. Problem-oriented languages have been developed for their needs. These languages do not require a detailed description of the algorithm. The user only needs to accurately describe the task and enter the appropriate data. The specified data is accepted by the program-generator, which provides the output data.

Problem-oriented languages are intended for solving specific classes of tasks, such as, for example, linear algebra, statistics, network planning, graph theory, etc. Examples of program-oriented languages are: MARS, ARIUS, PROZA, GRAPH, etc. We can even include the programming languages LISP and PROLOG, which are intended for solving problems of artificial intelligence, in this class.

As a rule, problem-oriented languages are the highest-level programming languages. This means that they depend the least on the technical characteristics of the computer on which the programs will later be executed.

Recently, the so-called script languages have been increasingly used. These are languages that are used for writing scripts - usually shorter programs that are, most often, integral parts of some applications. Script languages make up a special category of languages, and can belong to either procedural or problem-oriented languages.

It is clear that problem-oriented languages represent a strong support for digitalization.

1.2.3 Classification by area of application

Programs written in high-level programming languages are used in various areas. For problem-oriented languages, it is usually known which area they are intended for and where they give the best results. However, when it comes to procedural languages, the situation is not always clear because many were created with the pretension of being universal. However, some were designed in advance for specific purposes, while others have, over time, distinguished some areas in which they are most widely used and where, as a rule, they give the best results. Therefore, a classification of high-level programming languages can be made according to the area of application. This classification is probably the least precise, but useful for practice. Let us mention only some areas and the corresponding programming languages, although the list could be much more detailed.

- Learning programming: BASIC, Pascal, LOGO, …
- Business applications: SQL, COBOL, RPG, …

- Applications in mathematics: FORTRAN, ALGOL, …
- Applications in artificial intelligence: PROLOG, LISP, …
- Creating system software: C, Modula-2, …
- Development of parallel programs: Ada, CSP, OCCAM, …
- Development of visual applications: C++, Smalltalk, …
- Internet programming: Java, Perl, …

Many of the previously mentioned programming languages could be found in more than one class; here are highlighted the areas where their application is most well-known. Visual applications are particularly popular today, the development of which is enabled by: Visual BASIC, C++, Smalltalk, Java, C#, etc. It is clear that visual applications are created for various areas, which means that these languages are also applied in various areas.

1.2.4. Classification according to the method of solving the problem

Already after the appearance of the first higher-level programming languages, people tried to make programming languages as close as possible to the natural language of man. In such languages, the primary description of the procedure (algorithm) based on the use of commands should not be. Therefore, such languages are called non-procedural programming languages. On the other hand, languages in which the procedure described by a series of commands is used are called procedural or imperative. The essential difference between these two classes of programming languages is in the method of solving the problem.

In procedural programming languages, it is always necessary to describe HOW the problem is solved. However, many believe that it is more natural to just describe the problem precisely, i.e. to tell the computer WHAT is being solved and for the computer to look for a solution itself. This should be made possible by non-procedural programming languages, which are also called descriptive because they only describe the problem. The words 'how' and 'what' are key in distinguishing between procedural and non-procedural languages.

Due to the architecture of most modern computers, a non-procedural programming language would have to have a built-in "mechanism" for solving problems. However, it is difficult to create a powerful non-procedural language for computers, whose work is based on procedures. This is also the reason why many non-procedural languages regularly contain some procedural elements.

Today, procedural programming languages are the most widespread. The class of procedural programming languages includes: Pascal, C, FORTRAN, Ada, Modula-2, … Non-procedural languages are usually divided into two classes: functional and logical. The most famous representatives of functional programming languages are: LISP (in numerous versions), ML, Miranda, Haskell, etc. The most famous representative of logical programming languages is PROLOG (in various versions), and there are also: KLO, Mandala. Oz, etc.

A special class is made up of object-oriented languages, which primarily have procedural features. However, these languages also contain non-procedural elements. This is especially true for object-oriented languages that originated from descriptive languages. Object-oriented programming languages include: Simula 67, Smalltalk, C++, Eiffel, Java, C#, etc.

Another classification of advanced programming languages is described in chapter 2. Here, the main criterion is the programming paradigm to which the language belongs.

References

[1] Tošić D.: Periods in History of Computers, Zbornik radova "LIRA'95", Novi Sad, 1995. 7-14

[2] Francesco Fusaro :Digitization, digitalization and digital transformation explained – understanding differences incl. examples, 2023, https://morethandigital.info/en/digitization-digitalization-and-digital-transformation-explained-understanding-differences-incl-examples/

[3] Miloslavov, Aleksei. (2018). "The early period of the "Digital revolution" from the point of view of intellectual history". 10.32008/NORDSCI2018/B1/V1/23..

[4] Economic Commission for Latin America and the Caribbean (ECLAC), Digital technologies for a new future(LC/TS.2021/43), Santiago, 2021.

[5] R. Sebesta: Concept of programming languages, Addison Wesley, (10. ed.), 2012.

[6] D. A. Watt: Programming language design concepts, John Wiley & sons, 2004.

[7] A. Kartelj, V. Filipović i D. Tošić: Objektno orijentisano programiranje – programski jezik Java-1, Univerzitet u Beogradu, Matematički fakultet, Beograd, 2023.

[8] Tošić D.: Pascal-osnovi programiranja, Studentski trg, Beograd, 1977.

2.
CLASSIFICATION OF COMPUTER LANGUAGES AND THEIR ROLE IN DIGITALIZATION[1]

Abstract. The paper proposes a classification that includes all computer languages. The connection of each class with digitalization was considered. Thus, we can distinguish two large classes: Programming Languages and Domain Specific Language (DSLs). In the first class, two subclasses: low-level languages and high-level languages are further distinguished. Since high-level languages are the most numerous, we paid special attention and classify them into classes based on the dominant programming paradigm that they support. In the DSLs class (which contains a large number of diverse languages), we singled out markup and query languages because of their prevalence and importance for digitalization. The third subclass, within DSLs, consists of all other DSLs.

Keywords. classification, computer languages, digitalization.

1. Introduction

Modern computers are tightly coupled with a variety of languages ranging from machine language (built on a binary alphabet) to natural human languages. A large number of different computer languages have been created so far. So, it is useful to classify them somehow. There are various classifications of computer languages ([1], [2], [4], [5]). Thus, all computer languages can be divided into 2 classes: programming languages and domain-specific languages (Fig. 1). It is not easy to make a strict boundary between these classes. For example, the XSLT language is used to operate with XML data, i.e. it has the role of a programming language, but it is used within the framework of XML technology and therefore belongs to the class DSLs. Similarly, the UML language is primarily used for modeling, but can also take on the role of a programming language when used for a specific platform. Therefore, it is understandable that some authors classify these languages as programming moreover, we will make difference. Within programming languages, we will distinguish between:

[1]The content of this chapter is taken from the work: Dušan Tošić: CLASSIFICATION OF COMPUTER LANGUAGES USED FOR DIGITALIZATION, Review of the NCD 46 (2025), pp. 41–46

low-level languages and high-level languages. This division is accepted by almost all authors. Among the most used (most well-known) computer languages are high-level programming languages. As there are many of these languages [3], there is a need to classify them separately. They are often divided into procedural and declarative languages. However, this division is neither precise (most declarative languages contain procedural elements), nor comprehensive. A classification of high-level programming languages can be made based on the dominant programming paradigm that the language supports. However, some programming languages support two or more programming paradigms (for example, Python) so even this classification is not precise enough. Meanwhile, if the dominant paradigm is chosen, we can recognize 7 classes of high programming languages: procedural, concurrent, functional, logical, object-oriented, script and visual. (Fig.1). Some of these classes are important for digitalization, while some are less important. The role of each of these classes in the digitalization process is discussed further.

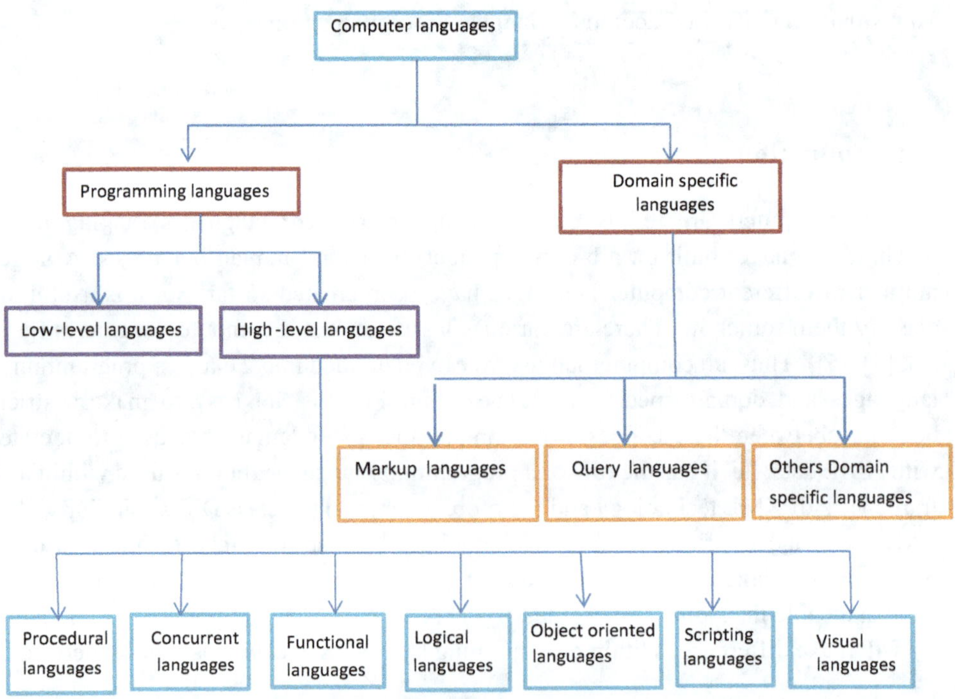

Fig.1. Classification Computer languages

2. Related work

Various classifications of computer languages can be found on the Internet and in computer books, depending on the classification criteria ([5], [15]). As high-level programming languages are the most important, their classifications are most often encountered [7]. The role of high-level programming languages in the digitalization process was discussed in the paper [9] by selecting the most popular programming languages of certain periods and analyzing their role in digitalization. In the paper [8] the role of XML technologies in the digitalization process is described. Papers [10] and [11] show in more detail the capabilities of XML technologies in digitalization.

3. Programming languages and digitalization

At the end of the Second World War, electronic digital computers supplanted analog computers and it could be said that the first steps towards digitization were made then. At the beginning of the development of digital computers, low-level programming languages were used, i.e. machine, assembly and macro languages. In this period, all processing on computers was realized with the help of these languages, and this is their contribution to digitalization. However, today they are completely supplanted by high-level programming languages. So, we will not consider their role in digitalization. Low-level languages are unsuitable for humans, so scientists tried to create a language that would be comfortable for humans, i.e. a language close to human spoken language and independent of the specific type of computer. The development tree of high programming languages is presented in the paper [9]. The characteristics of the most prominent high programming languages, created so far, are described, as well as the impact of each of them on the digitalization process. A large number of advanced programming languages were created by forcing one or more programming paradigms [6], [7]. It is, therefore, convenient to classify these languages based on the dominant paradigm that they support. Here we will list the most famous languages of the existing programming paradigms, as well as, their impact on the digitalization process.

3.1. Procedural language

The first programming paradigm is procedural. Some authors recognize the imperative and structural sub-paradigm within the procedural paradigm. The basic concept of both sub-paradigms is procedure (hence the name procedural), and the main difference appears in the use of the GOTO command. With the structural subparadigm, the use of the GOTO command is limited. Prominent programming languages of the imperative sub-paradigm are: FORTRAN, COBOL, ALGOL 60, ... The main languages of the structural sub-paradigm are: Pascal and C. The procedural paradigm is essential for digitalization. The most important software supporting digitalization written is using FORTRAN and C-language.

3.2 Concurrent languages

Concurrent paradigm (parallel) is close to procedural. Programming languages that support parallel processing are: PL/I, ALGOL 68, Ada, Concurrent Pascal, ...In these languages, the emphasis is on handling parallel processes and faster processing of large amounts of data. They are not necessary for digitalization, but they contribute to faster processing and efficient use of computer resources. It should be noted that the first languages of this paradigm (mentioned previously) are less used - they have been pushed out by modern languages such as Java and C# which also support parallel processes.

3.3. Functional languages

The functional paradigm emerged quickly after the procedural one. The first language of this paradigm was LISP, in which operations are performed by processing lists. In addition to LISP (which probably has the most descendants such as: NIL, MACLISP, Common LISP ...) the following languages are also based on this paradigm: FP, ML, Scheme, Iswim, Miranda, Haskell ... The basic concept of the functional paradigm is a function. Soon after its creation, LISP was recognized as an artificial intelligence language and many promoters of LISP assured users that the main problems of artificial intelligence would be solved by LISP. That did not happen, and interest in LISP and functional languages is rapidly declining. The functional paradigm becomes relevant again with the advent of PROLOG and by development of purely functional languages such as Haskell. LISP was used to develop various artificial intelligence applications, but also to create software packages: MATHEMATICA, AutoCad, etc. Bearing in mind these facts, we can conclude that functional languages are still successfully used and have played a significant role in the digitalization process.

3.4. Logical languages

Logical paradigm was created at the beginning of the seventies of the twentieth century. The main language of this paradigm was and remains PROLOG. Apart from PROLOG, the following languages are also based on the logical paradigm: Absys, Datalog, ASP, CLP, ILOG, Solver, ParLog, LIFE,… .PROLOG was created on the predicate calculus of the first order, and the other languages of this paradigm are also based on mathematical logic. In these languages, the main activity is the description of relations between objects. When PROLOG was created, it was bombastically announced as "the machine language of 5th generation computers". However, it did not fulfill that role. This is also the reason why interest in the logical paradigm has weakened. Nevertheless, the role of PROLOG is significant because it made possible to easily solve the problems of artificial intelligence. Also PROLOG stimulated interest in functional languages when it was realized that the solutions in PROLOG can also be implemented in functional languages. Otherwise, logical languages support digitalization, but their influence here is not of great importance.

3.5. Object-oriented languages

The object-oriented paradigm with the scripting paradigm is dominant today. This paradigm was created in the seventies of the 20th century, but unlike the logical one, it was slow to make its way. With the appearance of the language SmallTalk-80, it became known to the general public. The basic concept of this paradigm is an object. Objects are dynamic and interact with each other by exchanging messages. The programming languages that support this paradigm are: Simula 67, SmallTalk, C++, Eiffel, Java, C#,... The original language of this paradigm was Simula 67, but its main promoter was the SmallTalk language. With the advent of C++ and then Java, this paradigm became dominant. By using the language of this paradigm, digitalization is well supported and accelerated. Many scripting languages (such as Python, JavaScript, Ruby, PHP, ...) support this paradigm too.

3.6 Scripting languages

The scripting paradigm is probably the most contested. A large number of authors recognize scripting languages, but not the scripting paradigm as a separate programming paradigm. Unlike other paradigms, there is no essential concept that characterizes all its languages. Scripting languages are expanding - most of them are closely connected to the Internet and will be more and more popular in the future. A script is a list of commands that can be executed without user intervention, that is, without interaction with the user. In other words, a script is a program written in a scripting language. Script-languages often possess the features of programming languages of other paradigms, such as: object oriented, procedural, functional,...So this is also the reason why the scripting-paradigm is not recognized as a separate paradigm. Some of the script languages are: JavaScript, PHP, Perl, Python, AutoLISP, VBScript,...These languages are of great importance for digitalization and are intensively used in the digitalization process.

3.7. Visual languages

The visual paradigm is based on the use of diagrams instead of text, so it is also known as the diagrammatic, i.e. graphic programming paradigm. The basic building elements of the program are blocks and arrows. Blocks are a kind of objects, and arrows are used to connect blocks. Visual languages are used for educational purposes, for programming video games, for operating with multimedia, etc. Some of visual languages are: Alice, Flowcode, StartLogo, Dynamo, Nodal, Analytica, etc. We also include UML in Visual languages, although it is primarily a modeling language. When combined with Model Driven Architecture, UML becomes a visual language and can be said that it supports the visual paradigm. The Visual Basic, Visual C#, Visual J# etc. languages of the Microsoft Visual Studio and are not visual programming languages even though they have the attribute visual in the name. It cannot be said that visual languages have great importance for digitalization.

4. Domain-specific languages (DSLs)

While most programming languages aim to be general-purpose, DSLs are applied to solve problems within a specific domain ([12], [16]). DSLs are more often used within a program package (for example Matlab, Matcad, AutoCad, …) which also determines the application domain. The domain can be very narrow. For example, in finance, the following DSLs are used: AxLang, CPL, DAML, ... which are useful only to some people from financial circles. In terms of their characteristics, these languages are close to script languages. DSLs, in contrast to programming languages, aim to be: less comprehensive, much more expressive in their domain and convenient to eliminate redundancy. There are many areas of application of computer languages and we will not list them all (such a classification loses its meaning), but we will single out two classes of languages whose domains are very widespread. We are talking about Markup and Query languages whose domains are the Internet and databases. Some forms of programming appear in all these languages, so some authors classify them as programming languages [15]. However, their essential characteristic is that they originated and are tied to one area. Therefore, we classified them in the DSL class. Excluding Markup and Query languages, we classified all other DSLs into one class. Some of these languages can be very specific and can only be called from certain software, such as the MASH language. A lot of them are more widely distributed such as LaTex. DSLs can be combined with each other and even with programming languages.

4.1 Markup languages

With the advent of the Internet, digitalization gains even more importance. An important role for the expansion of digitization is played by the www (World Wide Web), whose popularity is due to the markup language HTML. However, HTML did not make it possible to use all the possibilities of the Internet. Therefore, the W3C group (http:/www.w3c.org) was created, which had the task of enabling the maximum use of the Internet while forming standards for presenting data on the internet. XML (eXtensible Markup Language) is markup language, which is a meta-language for creating other languages. XML enables digitization, and the languages created from it are suitable for digitalization. Nowadays, it is difficult to imagine digitization without XML. XML has become the development of a new technology that is intensively used on the internet. More about digitization and XML technologies can be found in the paper [8], and we will not consider more this technology and XML here.

4.2. Query languages

Query languages are related to databases, so they are also known as database query language (DQL). A database is an organized collection of structured information, or data. The database is managed by a database management system (DBMS). The DBMS enables the data to be easily accessed, managed, modified, updated, controlled, and organized. Query language is used to operate data (by means of DBMS), i.e. to query, manipulate, and define data. The most famous query languages are: SQL (Structured Query Language), NoSQL (Non-Structured Query Language), GraphQL, SPARQL, XQuery, Cypher, DMX (Data Mining Extensions), MDX (Multidimensional Expressions), etc. The digitization of databases began in the 60s of the 20th century, and intensive digitalization began with the appearance of query languages. Starting in the 80s of the last century, the most important query language was SQL, but in recent years it has been supplanted by NoSQL.

5. Conclusion

A large number of different languages is used on modern computers, so there is a need for their classification. We have classified them all into two classes: Programming and Domain Specific Languages. Programming languages can be further divided into low and high. Low programming languages are rarely used and we are not considered them. Contrary, high languages are intensively used and we proposed a classification based on the dominant programming paradigm they support. When it comes to DSLs ([13], [14]), there are a large number of domains in which they are used (word processing, finance, mathematics, creating computer games, ...) and it does not make sense to list them all. We have singled out only 2 domains: internet and databases, that related to Markup and Query languages. These languages are of great importance for both: digitization and digitalization.

References

[1] Alan Mycroft: Concepts in Programming Language, Computer Labarator, niversity of Cambridge, 2015 , http://www.cl.cam.ac.uk/teaching/1415/ConceptsPL/

[2] Jiy. Epözdemir: Programming Language Categories, 2024, https://medium.com/@jepozdemir/programming-language-categories-6b786d70e8f7.

[3] 10 Best Programming Languages to Learn in 2025. https://www.hostinger.com/tutorials/best-programming-languages-to-learn

[4] Introduction of Programming Paradigms,https://www.geeksforgeeks.org/introduction-of-programming-paradigms/, 2024

[5] R. Sebesta: Concept of programming languages, Addison Wesley, (7. ed.), 2006.

[6]Golding, S. A . Smolka and P. Wegner, Interactive Computation: The New Paradigm, Springer Verlag, 2006.

[7] S. Barry Cooper, Benedikt Löwe, and Andrea Sorbi: New Computational Paradigms: Changing Conceptions of What is Computable, Springer, 2007

[8] Tošić D.: "XML-tehnologije i digitalizacija", Pregled nacionalnog centra za digitalizaciju, 3, (2003), pp. 1-12.

[9] Tošić D.: ROLE OF PROGRAMMING LANGUAGES IN DIGITALIZATION, Review of the NCD 44 (2024), pp. 28–37.

[10] Tošić D., Filipović V. i Kratica J. : Using SVG – XML for representation of historical graphical data, Review of the National Center for Digitilization , 9 (2006), 39-45

[11] Tošić D., Filipović V, Tuba M. and Kratica J.: Potential Role of SMIL in Digitalization of National Heritage, Review of the National Center for Digitalization, 10 (2007), 33-39.

[12] Deursen, Arie & Klint, Paul & Visser, Joost. (2000). Domain-Specific Languages. ACM SIGPLAN Notices. 35. 26-36. 10.1145/352029.352035.

[13] Igor R. Alves: Making your life easier with domain-specific languages (DSLs), 2023, https://medium.com/wearewaes/making-your-life-easier-with-domain-specific-languages-dsl-1838d351d35

[14] Federico Tomassetti: The complete guide to (external) Domain Specific Languages, 2024, https://tomassetti.me/domain-specific-languages/

[15] Peslak A.: Computer programming languages in 2020: what we use, who uses them, and how do they impact job satisfaction, Issues in Information Systems, Volume 21, Issue 2, pp. 259-269, 2020.

[16] Domain-spec. language, https://en.wikipedia.org/wiki/Domain-specific_languag

3.
ROLE OF PROGRAMMING LANGUAGES IN DIGITALIZATION[2]

Abstract. The first high-level programming language was FORTRAN and was created in 1957. Since then, a large number of programming languages have been created. The time of creation of some of them, as well as their mutual relationship, can be described by a genealogical tree. On the genealogical tree that we used, 4 periods in the development of programming languages were distinguished, and in each period several of the most important languages were chosen. 14 most significant programming languages were selected (as chosen by the author of this work), and the main criterion was: popularity and influence on development of other languages. For each of the selected languages, some characteristics are briefly mentioned, as well as their importance for digitalization.

Keywords. programming languages, digitalization, genealogical tree.

1. Introduction

Today, digitalization is present in all human activities. What do we mean by digitalization? According to wikipedia [1] "digitalization may refer to: digital transformation, the adoption of digital tools to create new or modify existing products, services and operations". Digital transformation is based on digitization - the conversion of analog information into a digital format. There is a difference between digitalization and digitization. By digitization, content from any medium is transferred into a digital form, usually expressed by binary digits 0 and 1 [2]. Conversion does not change the content downloaded from the medium, it is just written differently. Digitalization means to change business processes over to use digital technologies. For digitalization, it is important to operate with data in digital form, which is done through digital transformation. Digital transformation is realized by electronic (digital) computers, often using a programming language. So far, a large number of programming languages (several thousand) have been created, many of which are dead (no longer used). However, a large number of programming languages have been successfully used in the digitalization process, and a significant number of them are

[2] The content of this chapter is taken from the work; . Dušan Tošić: ROLE OF PROGRAMMING LANGUAGES IN DIGITALIZATION, Review of the NCD 44 (2024), pp. 28–37.

still in use today. Following the development of programming languages from their origin until today, we will consider the impact of some of the most important (in the author's opinion) on the digitalization process.

2. Beginning of digitalization

It is difficult to say exactly when digitalization started. First steps towards digitalization were made in the 1940s, when digital computers supplanted analog ones. In that period, one cannot talk about digitalization as it is understood today, that is [3] "the ongoing integration of digital technologies and digitized data across the economy and society". Computer equipment is essential for digitalization. The first computers were very expensive and could only be owned by large companies and institutions. In this period, there were no conditions for digitalization even in developed countries. With the advent of mini computers, the situation improved, computers became cheaper and could be purchased by smaller companies and organizations. The use of mainframes (IBM/360, S370, Unisys, Cyber, ...) and minicomputers created better conditions for digitalization. Now we can already talk about the beginning of digitalization. However, digitalization flourished with the appearance of microcomputers, especially PCs. This is the period when every individual can get a computer and use information from the digitalization process.

3. Digitalization and languages

Language is a set of rules for communication between two or more subjects. Language is used to present and transmit information. All languages can be classified into two categories: natural and artificial. Natural languages are used for communication between people in spoken or written form. Artificial languages are created for use in certain areas where the use of natural languages is not suitable. Artificial languages include programming languages. Programming languages serve primarily for communication between humans and computers (sometimes it is also used for communication between people!) There is no strict (mathematical) definition of a programming language. However, there are various descriptive definitions. Thus, we can define a programming language as a set of syntactic and semantic rules used for the description (definition) of computer programs. What impact does digitalization have on languages, in general, and especially on programming languages? There is a large number of works on the relationship between language and digitalization. We will mention only two here. In the paper [4], the effect of digitalization on language and culture is considered. In the paper [5] the impact of digitalization on natural languages is considered. It is concluded that the impact is significant, but also different for different age categories. This could be expected because of the emergence of new technology regularly significantly affects natural languages (for example, the appearance of the automobile has influenced natural languages to be enriched with a number of new terms.) However, programming languages are directly involved in the digitalization process, so the impact of digitalization on programming languages is much more pronounced.

3.1. Programming languages

In order to make it easier to understand the terminology used here, we will list some commonly known terms related to programming languages. For a more detailed introduction to these concepts see [6] and [15]. A programming language can also be defined as an artificial language for describing constructions that can be translated into machine language and executed by a computer. Electronic computers can only execute constructions expressed using the binary alphabet, i.e. 0 and 1. A language created over a binary alphabet is called a machine language. Different types of computers use different machine languages. Machine languages are not suitable for humans, so languages similar to natural languages were created for writing programs. These are programming languages and all of them can be classified into 2 categories: machine-dependent and machine-independent languages. Machine-independent languages are also called high level programming languages. The first digital computers used exclusively machine-dependent languages. After the appearance of the first high level programming language, machine-dependent languages are used less and less, and a whole series of new high level languages have been created. In the further text, we will consider only high-level programming languages (some authors make a distinction between classical programming languages (FORTRAN, Pascal, Java, ...) and script languages. However, we will treat these languages in the same way).

Programming languages differ based on their characteristics (simplicity, expressiveness, uniformity, portability, efficiency, ...), but all programming languages are unique (unambiguous), unlike natural ones. In order to make a programming language with the best features, a large number of programming languages have been created. New languages are made by using previously created ones and taking their good features. Genealogical trees (Fig. 1.) are used to display the time of origin, as well as the mutual connections between laguages. Views of the connections between programming languages for different authors are different and therefore there are various genealogical-trees [7]. In order to highlight the most important programming languages, we will use the diagram from the site [8]. We distinguish 4 periods in the development of programming languages (see Fig. 1.) the period of

- first programming languages,
- programming languages of the Middle Ages,
- programming languages created at the end of the 20th century and
- future programming languages.

In each of the mentioned periods, several of the most important programming languages (according to the author's opinion) have been singled out and these languages are colored in different colors (yellow color is used for languages of the first generation, red for languages of the second period, etc.)

3.2. Script and markup languages

A scripting language is a programming language used for writing scripts. A script is a list **of commands that can be executed without user intervention, that is, without interaction with the** user. A script is a program written in a scripting language. Script languages are most often used to connect components within an application. They are often used in graphic environments. Some of the scripting languages are: JavaScript, PHP, Perl, Python, AutoLISP, VBScript.

An important role for the digitization process is played by markup languages, such as: SGML, HTML, XML. In parallel with the development of markup languages (especially XML), specialized programming languages have been developed for various processing related to markup languages. More about for markup languages, see [9]. We will not deal with markup languages here.

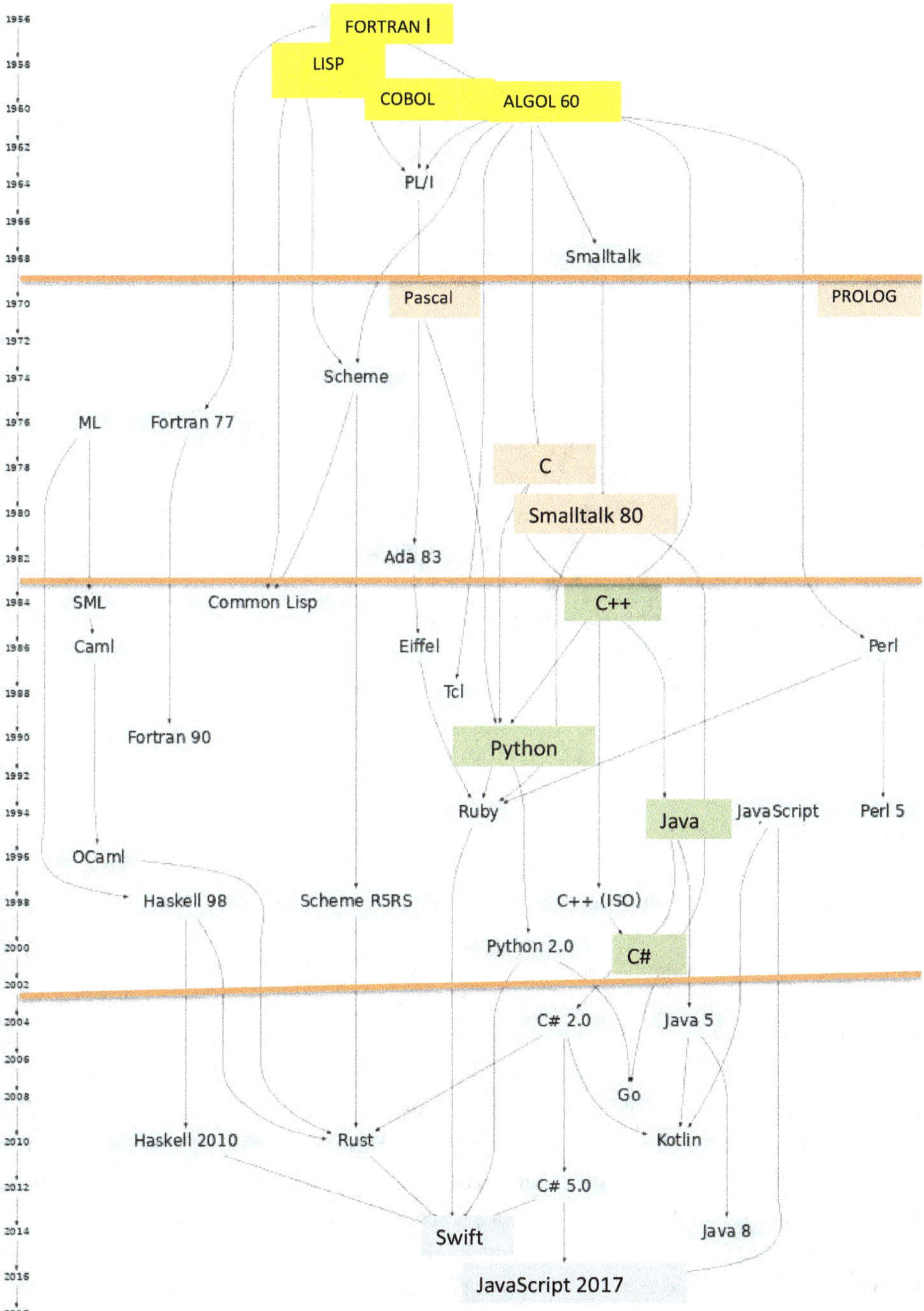

Fig. 1. Genealogical-tree of programming languages

4. First programming languages and digitalization

In the period when the first high-level programming languages were created, there were no conditions for digitalization (insufficient number of computers, absence of internet). Therefore, programming languages from this period could not support digitalization explicitly. However, through them, the ground was prepared for the future digitalization process, and therefore they deserve to consider their role. The first high-level programming language was FORTRAN [10]. The name FORTRAN is derived from FORmula TRANslation. It is a language created by a team of developers led by John Backus at IBM. It is intended for scientific research based on numerical calculations. After the first version of FORTRAN, several new ones appeared soon. The existence of various versions influenced that the problem of transferring programs from one computer to another appears. Therefore, in 1962, the American Standards Association established a committee with the task of proposing a FORTRAN standard. Starting with FORTRAN 66 and ending with FORTRAN 2023, several versions were proposed and with each new proposal the language was enriched according to new scientific achievements in this area. This has made FORTRAN one of the most vital and widely used programming languages. It is estimated that in the 1960s year of the 20th century, about 70% of computers in the world had a FORTRAN compiler. Thanks to the support of powerful corporations, many software packages from various fields have been created. A large number of them are still in use today. There is no mention of digitalization support by FORTRAN. FORTRAN was primarily used for numerical processing, while other types of processing (important for digitalization) were less common. It is possible that newer versions of FORTRAN were used for some applications, when digitalization began, but new languages that better supported digitalization were already in use.

In this period, it was considered that there should be special languages for mathematical and technical applications (such as FORTRAN) and special ones for business applications such as COBOL. The name COBOL is an acronym for COmmon Business Oriented Language and was implemented under the leadership of Grace Murray Hopper. COBOL has long been the leading language for business processing. COBOL contains a number of bad constructs and therefore it is not comfortable to use. According to recommendations of well-known experts in computing, this language is no longer used (it is not taught at colleges, it is not supported by modern literature, ...), although some applications developed in COBOL are still in use. There is no targeted support for digitalization in COBOL, but it can be said that the first steps towards digitalization are done in COBOL. Applications for: credit card transaction, traffic signals, phone calls etc. developed using COBOL are significant for the digitalization process. An important programming language from this period is LISP, which was created under the direction of John McCarthy [11]. The name LISP is derived from the LIStProcessing. As the name suggests, LISP is used for list processing. LISP promoted a functional style of programming - operations in it are based on the mathematical notion of function. Immediately after its creation, it was recognized as the language of Artificial Intelligence (AI for short). After initial success in solving some problems, the creators and users of LISP pretended to use LISP to solve all the most important problems of AI. Later theoretical results on NP-complete problems showed that this was not possible, which contributed to the decline in popularity of LISP. After that, LISP was operated only in some research centers, without wide acceptance. LISP became relevant again with the advent of PROLOG. Namely, it turned out that everything that can be done in PROLOG can also be done in LISP. As LISP was an American product, many American programmers began to return to LISP. (Thus, LISP was used in the creation of well-known software packages, such as: Mathematica, AutoCad, etc.) LISP is the language that probably has the most descendants [12]. Some AI problems solved in LISP are essential for digitalization. Therefore, it can be said that LISP is more significant for digitization compared to other languages of this period. LISP (some versions of it) is still used today, often in combination with scripting languages.

Another important language from this period is ALGOL 60 (Naur et al. 1960). This language is produced by a group of experts, half nominated by ACM and half by various European institutions. ALGOL is an abbreviation of ALGOrithmic Language, which means that it is a language for describing algorithms. Due to the large number of "bad" (arithmetical if statement, go to statement, ...) constructions in FORTRAN, ALGOL 60 was created with the idea of replacing FORTRAN. However, ALGOL 60 never reached the popularity of FORTRAN - barely 20% of computers in the world had a compiler for ALGOL 60. So, how did ALGOL 60 become among the most popular programming languages in this period? As ALGOL 60 was created by top experts, many solutions were proposed in it, which were later implemented in ALGOL-60's descendant languages, such as: Pascal, C, Smalltalk, ... In this way, ALGOL 60 left a deep trace of development almost of all modern programming languages. ALGOL 60 did not directly influence digitalization, but it did through its successors.

5. Programming languages of the Middle Ages and digitalization

At the beginning of the 60s years of the 20th century, significant experience was gained in creating programming languages. The idea of creating a universal language appeared. The International Federation for Information Processing (IFIP, established in 1960) had founded a Working Group on ALGOL (WG 2.1) with the task that, using

ALGOL 60, form a proposal for a new language. The members of the group disagreed about the conception of the new language. Some thought that it should be a powerful language that would contain the good features of most of the existing programming languages. Based on this concept, ALGOL 68 was created. This language was cumbersome, difficult to learn and compile, and it is almost forgotten today. In addition to ALGOL 68, several programming languages were created with the same idea - to produce a universal programming language that would cover different fields. Such languages were PL/1 and PLANNER. They suffered a similar fate as ALGOL 68, although PL/1 was used longer thanks to the support of IBM.

The members of the second group (led by Niklaus Wirth) believed that the new language should be simple, easy to learn and translate. That is how the Pascal programming language was born [13], [14]. The features that adorn Pascal are: simplicity, expressiveness, efficiency, conciseness and comprehensibility. With Pascal, the structured style of programming was successfully promoted. There are a number of programming languages that are direct descendants of Pascal. One of the most famous is the Ada programming language, which enables parallel programming. Pascal was mostly used for educational purposes - for learning programming. Pascal did not directly significantly influence digitalization, but indirectly (through his descendants) it did.

Unlike Pascal, the popularity of the C programming language is not declining. Various studies show that C [16], [17], [18] is among the 5 most popular programming languages even today. C was developed in 1972 by Dennis Ritchie at Bell Labs for implementing the UNIX operating system [23]. From its inception until today, it has been used to create: operating systems, embedded systems, web environments by using the Common Gateway Interface, etc. It is enough to mention only these areas and it is immediately clear that C had a significant role in digitalization. C is a universal programming language and due to its good features it will certainly be used in the future.

In this period, the programming language PROLOG was created [20], [21]. PROLOG is based on mathematical logic, and its creators are Colmerauer and Roussel. PROLOG is a non-procedural programming language and it is suitable for solving AI problems. The Japanese have announced the creation of a 5th Generation computers in which PROLOG would play the role of a machine language. Unfortunately, such computers were not built, and interest in PROLOG declined. PROLOG did not significantly affect the digitalization process.

A team led by A. Kay worked on the development of the Smalltalk language at the Xerox company. When the Smalltalk-80 version [22] was created, it was clear that it was a valuable product that should be presented to the professional community. Through the language Smalltalk 80, a new Object-Oriented paradigm was proposed. The basic concept is an object. Programming is realized through a set of objects that interact with each other. Windows, thumbnails and icons are used intensively in the language, and a mouse is often used instead of a keyboard. The emphasis is on the graphical user interface. Programs written in Smalltalk are several times slower than those written in C. This is the main reason that Smalltalk was used on a small number of computers. The speed of computers is their most important property, so even the news brought by Smalltalk could not immediately influence the choice of language. However, these innovations are important for digitalization, so we can say that Smalltalk has significantly contributed to digitalization even though it was not directly used.

6. Programming languages created at the end of the 20th century and digitalization

Programming languages from this period are still the most commonly used today. All of them (or packages created using them) enable working with various documents, images, sounds, ... It can be concluded that these languages fully support digitalization. The C++ programming language was created as an object-oriented superstructure of the C language. Its creator is Stroustrap [24]. C++ supports procedural and object-oriented programming style. It is used in MS Office, Adobe Photoshop, and various types of high-performance software. Despite that, C++ is a complex language, it is accepted by professional programmers and according to various researches, it is one of the 5 most used programming languages all the time.

The emergence of the Java language, which was created at Sun Microsystems under the leadership of James Gosling [25], contributed a lot to the decline in popularity of the C++ language. Java is a universal, object-oriented language with C syntax, but simpler than C++. From its inception, it was oriented towards the Internet. By using Bytecode, Java programs are largely independent of the platform they run on. This is very important in the Internet era. Java is used for: web development, artificial intelligence, Android development, and enterprise software (from smartcards to space vehicles). It is enough to list these areas and understand how important they are to digitalization. Java is a compiler-interpreter language. Programs written in Java are slower than corresponding programs in C/C++, but that does not prevent it from being among the most popular programming languages for years. C# is a Microsoft product modeled on Java (although Microsoft claims that it is derived from C++ and Visual

Basic). The language is used in almost all Microsoft products and is seen primarily in developing desktop applications. The features of C# are defined by using a standard library adapted to the .NET platform.
The fourth, chosen language from this period is Python [26], [27] whose creator is Guido Van Rossu. Python is a universal script language suitable for: web and Internet development, scientific computation, database access, education, software and game development, etc. Python's popularity is contributed by its support for different programming styles. Python is a language on the rise and is becoming one of the most popular programming languages in the world. It is used by software companies Google, Facebook. Spotify,... It can be said that Python supports the cutting-edge technology in the software industry. Due to the mentioned features, Python has a significant role in the digitalization process.

7. Future programming languages and digitization

The question arises as to which programming languages are used the most nowadays. Languages created at the end of the 20th century are still the most popular today. They are joined by several script languages, among which JavaScript stands out. It is certain that in the near future the most important programming languages will be: C++, Java, C#, Python and JavaScript. These languages would not survive in competition with newly created ones if they were not constantly improving and adapting according to new trends. For example, the C++ language was modified in 2003, 2011, 2014, 2017 and 2020, and appropriate versions are obtained: C++03, C++11, C++14, C++17 and C++20. Java and C# have been improved in a similar way. Which programming language will be the most used is difficult to predict. Support for visualization, the Internet and digitalization will be crucial for the choice of programming language. Quantum computing will also influence the choice of programming language, as well as AI support.
Since its appearance, the popularity of the JavaScript language has grown. JavaScript [31] was created by Brendan Eich in 1995. It is universal, multi-paradigm programming language, supporting object-oriented, imperative and functional paradigm. JavaScript is used to create interactive web applications and games. There is no a modern browser without JavaScript support. JavaScript is primarily used on the client side in dynamic web applications. It can also be used on the server side, however, the PHP script language is used much more often on the server side. The JavaScript-PHP combination is often used in web applications.

We also included Swift as a promising programming language, although its popularity is not at the level of the previously mentioned ones. Swift appeared in 2014 and inherited the good features of the following languages: Objective e-C, Rust, Haskell, Ruby, Python and C#. It is intended only for Apple computers and that is one of its shortcomings. It can be used on cellular devices, cloud applications, desktop computing, etc. One of the promising languages is the language Go (or Golang) - a product of the company Google in 2007. It was created with the intention of replacing C, but to be less complex than C++. It is often used to create smartphone applications, design databases, cloud computing, etc. It is a language that is easy to learn, fast and efficient. Go is used by companies: Google, Uber, Twitch and others. Among the programming languages that will be used in the future, most experts also include script languages: PHP, Ruby, Perl, Scala and Groovy. We will not consider them here.

8. Related work

ERP (Enterprise Resource Planning) systems play a very important role in digitalization. It is about complex software created by using various programming languages. In the paper [28] various ERP systems and the programming languages used in them are considered. Paper [29] contains a description of the impact of digitalization on the choice of programming language. Paper [4] describes the impact of digitalization on language in general. The programming languages essential for digital transformation in Japan are listed in the paper [30]. Here, the emphasis is on the banking sector. On the Internet, one can find a large number of sites about the popularity of programming languages and their future. We will not list them here, but we point out that the popularity of a programming language depends significantly on its support to digitalization.

9. Conclusion

With the development of programming languages, their role in the digitalization process grew. On the genealogical tree of higher level programming languages, 4 periods are distinguished, and in each period several of the most famous languages (in the author's opinion) are selected. The contribution to digitalization for each of them is analyzed and some of their most important properties are listed. Some of these languages are directly involved in the digitalization process, while others are indirectly involved. At the time of the appearance of the first high level programming languages the concept of digitalization was not known (as we understand it today). Therefore, the languages of this period could not be directly included in the digitalization. Already the languages of the middle period (for example C) could be directly included. Almost all modern programming languages support digitalization.

References

[1] https://en.wikipedia.org/wiki/Digitalization

[2] https://www.walkme.com/glossary/digitalization/

[3] https://www.eurofound.europa.eu/en/topic/digitalisation

[4] Samsudin, Samsudin & Mujab, Syaiful & Safar, Muh & Munandar, Haris. (2023). The effect of digitalization on language and culture in management practice modern education. Lingua. 19. 135-150. 10.34005/lingua.v19i2.3131.

[5] Lidiia Oliinyk, Nataliia Romaniuk, Halyna Kuznetsova, Inna Horbenko, Nadiia Senchylo-Tatlilioglu, The impact of digital and internet technologies on language development, Eduweb, 2022, julio-septiembre, v.16, n.3. pp. 41-54.

[6] Stojković V. and Tošić D: Zbirka zadataka iz programiranja - programski jezik BASIC, Privredno-finansijski vodič, Beograd, 1982.

[7] https://github.com/stereobooster/programming-languages-genealogical-tree

[8] http://rigaux.org/language-study/diagram.html

[9] Tošić D.: "XML-tehnologije i digitalizacija", Pregled nacionalnog centra za digitalizaciju, 3 , (2003), pp. 1-12.

[10] Tošić D.:FORTRAN 77 - Zbirka rešenih zadataka, Tehnička knjiga, Beograd, 1989.

[11] Budimac Z., Ivanović M., Putnik Z. i Tošić D: LISP kroz primere, Institut za matematiku PMF- a, Novi Sad, 1991,

[12] Budimac Z., Ivanović M., Bađonski M. i Tošić D.: Programski jezik SCHEME, Univerzitet u Novom Sadu – PMF, 1998.

[13] Stojković V., Tošić D., Stojmenović I.: Programski jezik Pascal, Naučna knjiga, Beograd, 1990.

[14] Tošić D.: Pascal-osnovi programiranja, Studentski trg, Beograd, 1977.

[15] Tošic D. i Stojković V.: Programski jezik Pascal – zbirka rešenih zadataka, Tehnička knjiga, Beograd, 1991.

[16] Peslak A.: Computer programming languages in 2020: what we use, who uses them, and how do they impact job satisfaction, Issues in Information Systems, Volume 21, Issue 2, pp. 259-269, 2020.

[17] https://www.tiobe.com/tiobe-index/

[18] The Top Programming Languages 2023 - IEEE Spectrum.

[19] Steele G. L. and Gabriel R. P.: (1993), The Evolution of Lisp, in 'The Second ACM SIGPLAN Conference on History of Programming Languages (HOPL-II), Cambridge, MA, USA, ACM, New York, pp. 231-270.

[20] Alain Colmerauer and Philippe Roussel:The birth of Prolog, ACM SIGPLAN Notices, Volume 28, Issue 3. pp 37–52, https://doi.org/10.1145/155360.155362

[21] Tošić D. i Protić R.: PROLOG kroz primere, Tehnička knjiga, Beograd, 1991.

[22] Kay, A. C. (1993), The Early History of Smalltalk, in The Second ACM SIGPLAN Conference on History of Programming Languages (HOPL-II), Cambridge, MA, USA , ACM, New York , pp. 69--95

[23] Ritchie D. M.:. (1993), The development of the C Language, in 'The Second ACM SIGPLAN Conference on History of Programming Languages (HOPL-II), Cambridge, MA, USA, ACM, New York, pp.201-208.

[24] Stroustrupt B.: (1993):. A History of C++: 1979-191 in 'The Second ACM SIGPLAN Conference on History of Programming Languages (HOPL-II), Cambridge, MA, USA, ACM, New York, pp. 271-298.

[25] Kartelj A., Filipović V. i Tošić D.: Objektno orijentisano programiranje – programski jezik Java – 1, Matematički fakultet, Beograd, 2023.

[26] Miloš A. Kovačević: Osnove programiranja u Pajtonu, Građevinski fakultet u Beogradu, 20021.

[27] Eric Matthes: Python intenzivni kurs,Čačak, Kompjuter biblioteka, 2023.

[28] Zečević A., Đ. Stakić i D. Đurđić: The role and importance of programming languages in the application of ERP solutions, Ekonomika preduzeća 71 (7-8), 448-459, 2023.

[29] Starchikov C.: Digitalisation is the battlefield or how to choose your programming languages? 2020, https://www.linkedin.com.

[30] Digital Transformation in Japan: Revealing Top Programming Languages, Tntra, 2023, https://medium.com

[31] Marijn Haverbeke: JavaScipt elokventno, Stručna knjiga, 2019.

4.
MARKUP LANGUAGES AND DIGITIZATION

Markup languages are of great importance for digitization. They made it easier to represent and present various entities and therefore influenced the acceleration of the digitalization process.

A text markup language consists of a set of markers (tags) that are combined with the text in accordance with some rules, with the aim of describing the structure or appearance of the document expressed by the text.

We can say that text marking is the process of adding additional codes to the text, expressed electronically, in order to define its structure or format in which it will appear [1].

The most famous markup language is HTML (Hypertext Markup Language). Thanks to this language and the Internet, digitization has made a significant leap in its development. However, there are various other markup languages. The following examples show the layout of parts of documents in several active markup languages

1. LaTeX:

```
.................

\begin{center}

S A D R \v{Z} A J

\end{center}

\no

{\bf 1. Uvod}\\

1.1. Genetski i evolucioni algoritmi\\

1.2. O teoriji evolucije i zakonima genetike\\

1.3. Evoluciona izra\v{c}unavanja\\

\hspace*{1cm} 1.3.1 Genetski algoritmi\\
```

```
\hspace*{1cm} 1.3.2 Evolucione strategije\\

\hspace*{1cm} 1.3.3 Evoluciono programiranje\\

\hspace*{1cm} 1.3.4 Genetsko programiranje\\

.....
```

2. HTML

```
............

<ol> Moji omiljeni sportovi su:

  <li> Plivanje

  <li> Kosarka

  <li> Fudbal

  <li> Gimnastika

</ol>
```

3. RTF

```
..................

{\*\pnseclvl9\pnlcrm\pnstart1\pnindent720\pnhang {\pntxtb (}{\pntxta )}}\pard\plain
\ql \li0\ri0\widctlpar\aspalpha\aspnum\faauto\adjustright\rin0\lin0\itap0

\fs24\lang1033\langfe1033\cgrid\langnp1033\langfenp1033 {\insrsid16461327
Zdravo!

\par }}
```

4. XML

```
<?xml version="1.0"?>

<MEMO>

<TO> Marko Peric </TO>
```

<CC> Milos Arsic </CC>

<FROM>Dusan Tosic</FROM>

<DATE>03/16/99</DATE>

<RE>Novi kurs</RE>

<BODY>Sa zadovoljstvom Vas obavestavamo da smo otpoceli sa

novim kursom iz programskih jezika. Kurs bi trebalo da traje do kraja

letnjeg semestra. </BODY>

</MEMO>

Markup languages can be classified in various ways ([2], [3]). Thus, we can distinguish:

- presentational
- procedural and
- descriptive

markup languages.

Presentation languages visually express (present) the entire text without displaying the used markers (**Word, Rtf**, ...).

Procedural markup languages are also used for visual presentation of text, but markers are visible and additional software is needed to process unified text with markers. This type of language includes: **nroff, troff, TeX, PostScript...**

Descriptive markup languages combine markers (tags) and parts of text without having to present the text. SGML and XML are languages developed as general purpose descriptive languages. This includes various languages derived from XML**: MathML, SVG, SMIL,...,** but also various others: **TEI, Open eBook, XBRL, ...**

The HTML language contains descriptive elements ("blockquote" or "href=" attribute), but also procedural elements (<b>- tag)

Descriptive languages are characterized by flexibility - they describe "WHAT text elements essentially represent", not "HOW they will be displayed". Unlike these languages, presentational and procedural languages primarily serve to determine how the text will be presented.

There are a large number of descriptive languages for various fields of application (chemistry, aviation, marine, ...) and they are mostly based on XML. XML operates with documents, but an XML document is not easy to define. The W3C states: "XML documents are written in accordance with SGML documents". A document in SGML is: "a collection of information that is processed as a single unit"

What is SGML and how is XML related to SGML?

In the 1960s, Charles Goldfarb, Ed Mosher and Ray Lorie faced the problem of processing documents of different types at IBM. They decided to create a general document processing language. In order for the documents to be portable, they set 3 requirements:

1. Processing programs must support a common format

2. The common format is specific to the domain of legal documents

3. The format of documents must meet specific rules

For example, for a memorandum it is important:

• To whom the document is intended (the "To:" field)

• To whom the document is addressed (the "CC:" field)

• Who sent the document (the "From:" field)

• Date of writing the document (the "Date:" field)

• Subject of writing (answer) (the "Re:" field)

• Body of the document

Based on the set requirements, a document processing language was created and named GML (Generalized Murkup Language). In 1986, this language was standardized and named SGML (Standard Generalized Murkup Language).

In 1989, Tim Berners-Lee began creating a new HTML markup language. Due to its popularity on the Internet, HTML will contribute to the development of many other markup languages, primarily XML. In 1998, the W3C group proposed the introduction of a new (meta)-language: XML (Jon Bosak). Both languages (HTML and XML) use elements of SGML. Why SGML itself was not used, but new languages were developed? SGML is a complex language, difficult to learn and use. To avoid the fate of cumbersome and failed programming languages, new languages were created (using some elements of SGML).

4.1. About XML

XML (Extensible Markup Language is a set of rules for defining semantic tags (markers, tags) that break the document into parts and serve to identify various parts of the document [4], [5]. It is a meta-language for marking (markup) and serves to define the syntax through which other markup languages (specific to certain areas) will be defined. XML does not have fixed tags (like HTML, TeX, troff), but only defines some rules for organizing tags. (For example, in XML tag must start with < and end with > (arrow brackets), but XML doesn't say what names should be between these brackets. The following is a representation of a simple XML document:

```
<?xml version="1.0" encoding="UTF-8"?>

<document>

    <title> Greetings !</title>

    <message> Welcome to the XML course .</message>

</document>
```

An element is a basic component of XML. Everything is placed in the frame of the element. (In the previous example, the element is a *document*). Each opening tag must have its own closing tag. XML is case sensitive (<document> is different from <DOCUMENT>) unlike HTML. The element name must start with a letter or an underscore. Other symbols can be: letters, numbers, underscore, period and dash. Attributes can be found within an element (as in the initial declaration where the attribute *is version "1.0"*). Other elements, text, etc. can be specified between the element's start and end tags. (In our example the *<title>* and *<message>* elements.) All elements must be contained within a single 'general element' called the *root element*. (In our case it's an element named *<document>.)*

If we try to display the mentioned document using a browser, it will be displayed as it is written - without trying to interpret individual tags (there is no predetermined meaning for them). If we enter the previous content into the Prvi.xml file, and view it using IE, we get:

```
<document>
    <title> Greetings !</title>
    <message> Welcome to the XML course. </message>
</document>
```

In order to display the contents of this XML document in the 'right' way (without tags), we should use CSS (cascading style sheets) or XSL (Extensible Stylesheet Language). This is a good example of how to handle XML-related content, i.e. how XML-technology is formed. CSS is also used in HTML and some call it a special technology for defining the style that will be used to display content. To indicate that CSS will be used, we add:

```
<?xml-stylesheet type="text/css" href="Prvi.css"?>
```

This is the so-called processing instruction and tells the software (in this case, the browser) how to process the XML document. A processor instruction is surrounded by symbols <? and ?>. In order to execute the processor instruction, there should be a Prvi.css file with a description of the XML elements. The content Prvi.css file can be as follows:

```
title {display: block; font-size: 30pt; text-align: center}

message {display: block; font-size: 40pt;  text-align: center}
```

If we connect these two files with a processor instruction (the processor instruction is inserted into the Prvi.xml file) by specifying the Prvi.xml file, we get:

Greetings!

Welcome to the XML course.

The point in working with XML documents is not in the ability to display them, but in the ability to access each element and use the element in processing. To access XML elements, the JavaScript language can be used, as well as the Java language. The Java programming language has packages and a number of methods that support this type of processing. Suppose we want to extract the title element from the previous document. A Java program (written in the file Prvi.java) can look like this:

```
import javax.xml.parsers.*;

import org.w3c.dom.*;

import java.io.*;

public class Prvi

{

  static public void main(String[] argv)

  {

    try {

    DocumentBuilderFactory dbf =

      DocumentBuilderFactory.newInstance();

    DocumentBuilder db = null;

    try {

      db = dbf.newDocumentBuilder();

    }

    catch (ParserConfigurationException pce) {}

    Document doc = null;

      doc = db.parse("Prvi.xml");

      for (Node node = doc.getDocumentElement().getFirstChild();

        node != null; node = node.getNextSibling()) {

        if (node instanceof Element) {
```

```
            if (node.getNodeName().equals("title")) {
              StringBuffer buffer = new StringBuffer();
              for (Node subnode = node.getFirstChild();
                subnode != null; subnode = subnode. getNextSibling()){
                if (subnode instanceof Text) {
                  buffer.append(subnode.getNodeValue());
                }
              }
              System.out.println(buffer.toString());
            }
          }
        }
      } catch (Exception e) {
        e.printStackTrace();
      }
    }
}
```

Therefore, any element from the XML document can be extracted and operated with it.
The reader can learn more about XML technologies in Chapter 5.

Although XML is simple, it has contributed to the development of a number of new languages and software tools, thus creating a technology based on XML. We can even talk about more technologies based on XML. These technologies are no longer simple and their implementation is becoming complicated.

What is the outlook for XML and emerging technologies? The paper [6] states: "One of the latest trends in XML development is the adoption of standards such as XSD (XML Schema Definition) and XSLT (eXtensible Stylesheet Language Transformations) to facilitate interoperability between systems."

- XSD provides a way to define the structure of XML documents, allowing developers to validate data against a specific schema.

- XSLT enables developers to transform XML documents into different formats, making it easier to exchange data between systems that speak different languages."

In the paper [6], it is also stated that some other technologies are expanding (for example, JSON) and that they are suppressing XML technology in some areas.

References

[1] Brian Benz with John R. Durant: XML Programming Bible, Publisher: Wiley Publishing, Inc.,2003.

[2] Elliotte Rusty Harold: XML 1.1 Bible, 3rd Edition, Wiley Publishing, 2004.

[3] Elliotte Rusty Harold, W. Scott Means: XML in a Nutshell, 3rd Edition, Publisher: O'Reilly Pub. 2004.

[4] Erik T. Ray: Learning XML, 2nd Edition, Publisher: O'ReillyPub Date: September 2003.

[5] Steven Holzner: Sams Teach Yourself XML in 21 Days, Third Edition, Publisher: Sams PublishingPub Date: October 14, 2003.

[6] Vasile Crudu & MoldStud Research Team: What are the latest trends in XML development?, 2024.

5.
XML TECHNOLOGIES AND DIGITALIZATION[3]

Abstract. Since the group W3C (http:/www.w3c.org) is formed, for the purpose of working on making and proposing standards for representation the data for Internet, it is done a lot. First of all, the meta-language XML is described and after that the whole line of new technologies (XSLT, DOM, DDT, XHTML, XSL-FO, XML-Shema, SVG, ...), based on XML, is followed. If the representation of datain electronic form is planed for a durable period, the XML-technologies could not be avoided. All XML technologies are interesting and provide the great possibilities in describing national cultural inheritance. In this paper the role of XML is described and some XML technologies are presented.

1. Introduction

XML was conceived with the idea of enabling full utilization and interoperability of the World Wide Web. (see[4]) When the idea of its creation was born, probably not even the most optimists could have predicted the impact this product would have on the further development of information science and computing. XML (eXtensible Markup Language) is a metalanguage, which is used to describe other languages, and whose purpose can be different. Languages that are created using XML (in accordance with the rules of XML) are called XML applications. In a very short period of time, languages have been developed for displaying multimedia content, for describing presentations on the Internet, for displaying mathematical content, etc., which are based on XML. But not only that, various software tools have been developed for the application of these languages, rules for their application have been described and adjustments have been made to existing IT products. And while at the beginning it was possible to speak only of XML technology, after the application branched out, it is possible to speak of a whole range of XML technologies. Large software manufacturers (Microsoft, IBM, Sun, ...) very quickly realized the importance of XML technologies and their main products (Dot-net, Database Management Systems, Multi-tier applications, ...) are based on XML. This support is very significant because it contributes to the even greater popularity of XML technologies. With this in mind, any planning of data digitalization should be based on XML technologies. The choice of

[3] The content of this chapter is taken from the work: . Tošić D.: "XML-tehnologije i digitalizacija", Pregled nacionalnog centra za digitalizaciju, 3(2003), 1-12. The original work was written in Serbian. For the purposes of this book, it was translated into English.

these technologies is a guarantee that data will be easy to process, transform and use in the future.

2. WWW and W3C Standards

The name W3C is an abbreviation for World Wide Web Consortium. It is an organization formed in 1994 with the mission of: "leading the World Wide Web towards its full potential by developing common protocols that promote the continued growth of the network and ensure its interoperability" ([1]).

The early 1990s saw a rapid development of the Web. The basic language for describing data on the Web was HTML. Data described Web. The basic language for describing data on the Web was HTML. Data described using HTML could be easily displayed, but when it was necessary to operate on such data in any way, great difficulties arose. In order to make the Web dynamic, interactive and accessible to data, various attempts were made to supplement and modify HTML. This led to great diversity, and therefore to the impossibility of application on different platforms, difficulty in mastering various techniques, etc. In addition, various browser manufacturers (primarily Microsoft and Netscape) supplemented and modified the HTML language in various ways, not respecting many standards. There was a need to create standards in this area. In order for a standard to be accepted by a wide range of users and to be able to be maintained, it must be solidly based. Therefore, it was necessary to create a language with which data could be easily represented on the Web and from which it could be easily downloaded, i.e. with which it could be easily operated. That is why the W3C consortium was formed and as one of the first products of this expert body the meta-language XML was created. Already in the process of creating XML, it was understood that the problems the consortium faced were very serious and that they extended to various areas of computing. W3C members tackled these problems and as a result, various technologies have emerged, all of which are, in some way, related to XML.

The W3C is not a government organization, nor a paid international standards-making organization. Therefore, its products (documents) are not official standards, but recommendations. Although recommendations are not called standards, they are unofficial standards on the Web, and users are left to decide whether to follow these recommendations.

The most famous software companies (Microsoft, Adobe, Netscape, Sun, ...) participated in the creation of W3C, and very famous scientists and creators in the field of computer science participated (and still participate) in the development of recommendations. Any company (or individual) willing to get involved in the development of recommendations can become a member of the consortium. This means that it is an open organization whose work is represented by complete transparency. Everything that W3C has done so far can be "downloaded" from the Web and everything is free. Also, on the W3C sites (see [1] and [2]) you can see what's next, what's being worked on, and what the plans are for the future.

W3C is an international consortium located on three continents. The consortium's headquarters are located in North America, France, and Japan. Given the above, it can be said that the work of W3C is well-designed. The recommendations are not only unofficial standards, but also useful documents from which you can learn a lot about the Internet and XML technologies.

3. Why has XML become so popular?

The XML Recommendation was published in 1998 (see [3]) and describes version 1.0, which is still current. XML originated from SGML - a general and complex language for marking up data. SGML itself (Standard Generalized Markup Language) originated in 1986 by standardizing the GML (Generalized Markup Language), which was created in the 1960s and was created by Charles Goldfarb, Ed Mocher and Rau Lorie. XML is based on the same principles as SGML, but is much simpler and adapted to the Web.

Note that HTML also originated from SGML, but with much greater simplifications and modifications.

XML can be said to be a well-designed (meta)language. This is also the reason why it has launched a flood of new technologies. The number of rules for creating XML constructs is not large, and based on this, it can be concluded that it is a simple language. However, the contents included in XML (accompanying language elements), which are products of technologies related to XML, make it complex. This is where the main danger lies for further applications and expansion of XML. Namely, experience in the development of computer science has shown that everything that is overly complex (especially if it is difficult to learn) is abandoned, i.e. after a certain period it ceases to be relevant. If XML itself is simple enough, the question arises whether the accompanying technologies that make it complex are necessary. Without accompanying technologies, XML would not be expressive enough and would again lose its main purpose. (For example, XML has very limited capabilities for working with images and graphics. However, if you use scalable vector graphics (a new technology based on XML!), you get one of the most powerful tools for supporting graphics.)

XML is well structured and you can easily operate on objects in it. Data in XML is represented in the form of a tree structure, where each node in the tree can be treated as a separate object. By separating a node with all branches that originate from it, you practically separate one object that can be treated in the same way as objects in object-oriented languages. In this way, data described using XML can be relatively easily processed in an object-oriented languages. By introducing the concept of an entity, it is possible to treat objects of any type (graphics, tables, links, ...) in XML.

Since there are rules for describing data in XML, there are also tools (SAX, DOM, ...) that can be used to check whether the XML rules for describing data are respected. If these rules are satisfied in a document, then it is said to be a well-formed XML document. In order to apply XML technologies, the documents that are operated on must be well-formed. However, by using additional technologies (DTD, XML-Scheme, ...), in XML there is a possibility of checking the validity of the described data. What is achieved by this? Through data validation, additional data checks are performed regarding the fulfillment ofcertain requirements. This significantly reduces the possibility that the data being operated on will be incorrect. This in turn eliminates errors when using that data.

In XML, the emphasis is on data description. In general, XML and related technologies are characterized by descriptiveness. Through precise data description and validation, the possibility of using procedural tools is reduced. This facilitates the data processing process and reduces errors during processing.

XML is not tied to any specific platform. Data described in XML is independent of the platform on which it is used. Nowadays, when there are a large number of different types of computers (platforms) on the Internet, this feature is highly desirable. For many users, a major problem is the inability to use data on one platform because the data is adapted to another platform. With data described in XML, such problems are almost completely eliminated.

Therefore, it can be concluded that XML has a number of nice features. This is the reason why it has achieved great popularity in a short time (with supporting technologies). Due to the complexity of the supporting technologies, there is a danger (according to this author!) that a large number of users cannot easily adopt and accept XML. However, the authors of the entire concept believe that very complex problems (which are affected by XML) cannot be solved without using complex tools. For the description and use of data described using XML, it is not necessary to know all the supporting technologies, which is a facilitating circumstance.

4. XML technologies

The development of XML has initiated the development of a number of new technologies. Some of these technologies are in the early stages of development, while others are almost fully established. We will consider XML technology to be established if a corresponding recommendation has been issued for it. Here we will briefly describe some XML technologies, including their abbreviations.

Common Markup for Micropayment is a technology related to e-business and simplifying payments on the Web. **CSS (Cascading Style Sheets)** is a tool used to present data expressed in HTML and XML on the Web. Strictly speaking, this is not an XML technology, but a tool taken from HTML. **DOM (Document Object Model)** allows the processing of documents described using XML. **DTD (Document Type Definition)** imposes certain restrictions on XML elements (which tags are allowed, from which set the values are taken, ...). **P3P (Platform for Personal Privacy Preferences**) is a technology that allows to bypass sites with unwanted content. **PICS (Platform for Internet Content Selection**) allows labels (metadata) to be attached to Internet content. They are used to identify materials suitable for children. **RDF (Resource Description Framework)** refers to the operation of metadata. It is believed that RDF technology should contribute to a better understanding of data from the Web and facilitate its processing. **SVG (Scalable Vector Graphics)** is a relatively new technology and refers to vector graphics and animation. **SMIL (Synchronized Multimedia Integrated Language)** is, as the name suggests, related to the processing of multimedia documents**. XForms** is a developing technology. It is intended to provide an easy way to work with forms on the Web. **XHTML (Extensible Hypertext Markup Language**) is a language that represents an XML application and is used to describe data on the Web**. XIS** or **Infoset (XML Information Set)** is used to retrieve data from well-formed XML documents. XML **Query** is a technology that should enable the formation o queries for databases. These queries should be similar to queries in SQL. XML **Schema** should enable overcoming the shortcomings of DTD and enable a more precise description of data, i.e. data types. XML Signatures should be used to describe the syntax of documents that would allow any URI (Uniform Resource Indicator) on the Web to be easily referenced. XSL-FO (Extensible Stylesheet Language – Formatting Objects) has a similar role to CSS, i.e. it should enable the display o XML documents in a convenient way. Unlike CSS, this is a completely XML technology. XSLT (Extensible Stylesheet Language Transformations) is a language that allows you to transform an XML document into another form (for example, into an XHTML document).

A more detailed description of XML technology can be found in[5].

5. Representation and presentation of data using XML.

Here we will not describe XML and the way of recording documents in XML. However, we will describe how to transform an XML document in order to display it adequately on the Web. In doing so, we will demonstrate the use of some XML technologies. Let us have the following document described in XML (it is a famous poem by the Serbian poet Aleksa Šantić “Ne veruj …”

```
<?xml version="1.0" encoding="UTF-8" ?>
- <Pesma>
    <naslov>Ne veruj ...</naslov>
    <autor>Aleksa Šantić</autor>
    <datum>1905</datum>
  - <strofa>
      <red>Ne veruj u moje stihove i rime</red>
      <red>Kad ti kažu, draga, da te silno volim,</red>
      <red>U trenutku svakom da se za te molim</red>
      <red>I da ti u stabla urezujem ime ...</red>
    </strofa>
  - <strofa>
      <red>Ne veruj! No kasno, kad se mesec javi</red>
      <red>I prelije srmom vrh modrijeh krša,</red>
      <red>Tamo gde u grmu proleće leprša</red>
      <red>I gde slatko spava naš jorgovan plavi.</red>
    </strofa>
  - <strofa>
      <red>Dođi, čekaću te! U časima tijim,</red>
      <red>kad na grudi moje priljubiš se čvršće,</red>
      <red>Osjetiš li, draga, da mi t'jelo dršće,</red>
      <red>I da silno gorim ognjevima svijem,</red>
    </strofa>
  - <strofa>
      <red>Tada veruj meni, i ne pitaj više!</red>
      <red>Jer istinska ljubav za riječi ne zna;</red>
      <red>Ona samo plamti, silna, neoprezna,</red>
      <red>Niti mari, draga, da stihove piše!</red>
    </strofa>
  </Pesma>
```

When viewed in a browser, this document is displayed in a cluttered form because the tags are also displayed. How can a document be displayed in a more manageable form? One way is to transform it into an XHTML document. The transformation can be done using the XSLT language. The description of the transformation is given in a separate file with the extension XSL. Let it be the file Pesma.xsl with the following content:

```
<?xml version="1.0" ?>
- <xsl:stylesheet xmlns:xsl="http://njnjnj.nj3.org/1999/XSL/Transform" version="1.0">
  - <xsl:template match="Pesma">
    - <html>
      - <head>
        - <title>
            <xsl:value-of select="naslov" />
          </title>
        </head>
      - <body>
          <xsl:apply-templates select="naslov" />
          <xsl:apply-templates select="strofa" />
          <xsl:apply-templates select="autor" />
          <xsl:apply-templates select="datum" />
        </body>
      </html>
    </xsl:template>
  - <xsl:template match="naslov">
    - <div align="center">
      - <h1>
          <xsl:value-of select="." />
        </h1>
      </div>
    </xsl:template>
  - <xsl:template match="autor">
    - <div align="left">
      - <h2>
          <xsl:value-of select="." />
        </h2>
      </div>
    </xsl:template>
  - <xsl:template match="datum">
    - <div align="left">
      - <h2>
          <xsl:value-of select="." />
        </h2>
      </div>
    </xsl:template>
  - <xsl:template match="strofa">
    - <p>

        <xsl:apply-templates select="red" />
      </p>
    </xsl:template>
  - <xsl:template match="red">
      <xsl:value-of select="." />
      <br />
    </xsl:template>
</xsl:stylesheet>
```

To obtain a document in a more readable form, a processor (program) is needed that transforms the XML document into an XHTML document. The Saxon processor can be used for this purpose (see [6]). The translation process is implemented with the command (from DOS):

>saxon Song.xml Song.xsl > Song.html

The XHTML document Song.html is formed and displayed in the following way:

Не веруј ...

Не веруј у моје стихове и риме
Кад ти кажу, драга, да те силно волим,
У тренутку сваком да се за те молим
И да ти у стабла урезујем име ...

Не веруј! Но касно, кад се месец јави
И прелије срмом врх модријех крша,
Тамо где у грму пролеће лепрша
И где слатко спава наш јоргован плави.

Дођи, чекаћу те! У часима тијим,
кад на груди моје приљубиш се чвршће,
Осјетиш ли, драга, да ми т'јело дршће,
И да силно горим огњевима свијем,

Тада веруј мени, и не питај више!
Јер истинска љубав за ријечи не зна;
Она само пламти, силна, неопрезна,
Нити мари, драга, да стихове пише!

Алекса Шантић 1905

The document displayed in this way is much more clear. There are other ways to make an XML document more clear. For example, if we use CSS technology, we need to create a file with the extension css that contains a description of each element from the XML document. Let it be the file Pesma.css with the following content:

```
naslov{
  display: block;
  margin-bottom: 10px;
  font-family: Arial, Helvetica;
  color: red;
  text-decoration: underline
  }
autor{
  display: block;
  margin-bottom: 5px;
  font-family: Arial, Helvetica;
  color: blue
  }
datum{
  display: block;
  margin-bottom: 15px;
  font-family: Arial, Helvetica;
  color: blue
  }
red{
  display: block;
  margin-bottom: 5px;
  color:green;
  }
strofa{
  display: block;
  margin-bottom: 20px;
  ;}
```

If we have a file formatted like this, we need to make a change in the original XML- document by adding one line (after the first line) of the form:

<?xml-stylesheet type="text/css" href="pesma.css" ?>

By viewing the document **Pesma.xml** using a browser, we get the output of the form:

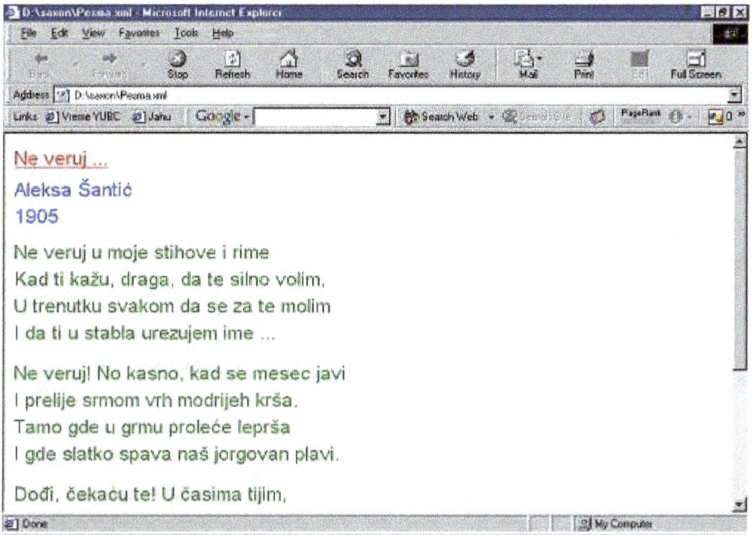

6. Using Serbian letters in XML documents

XML is based on Unicode. This means that various characters can be used in documents, you just need to know their codes. Unicode values for various sets of characters (including Cyrillic) can be found on the Web (see [7]). In the previous example, the beginning of the text version of the XML document looks like this:

```
<?xml version='1.0' encoding='UTF-8'?>

<Pesma>
<naslov>Ne veruj ...</naslov>
<autor>Aleksa &#352;anti&#263;</autor>
<datum>1905</datum>

<strofa>
<red>Ne veruj u moje stihove i rime </red>
<red>Kad ti ka&#382;u, draga, da te silno volim, </red>
..........................................
```

It is noted that Unicode codes are used for the letters Ш, ћ and ж. (These codes start with the symbols &# and end with a semicolon (;). If they are in hexadecimal form, they start with the characters &#x.) If we want to use Cyrillic in a document, the processing principles remain the same, only the codes for the letters in the document change. Let the beginning of our document (in text form) look like this:

```
<?xml version='1.0'  encoding='UTF-8'?>
<Pesma>
<naslov>&#x41D;&#x435;  &#x432;&#x435;&#x440;&#x443;&#x458;  ...</naslov>
<autor>&#x410;&#x43B;&#x435;&#x43A;&#x441;&#x430;
&#x428;&#x430;&#x43D;&#x442;&#x438;&#x45b;</autor>
<datum>1905</datum>
<strofa>
<red>&#x41D;&#x435;  &#x432;&#x435;&#x440;&#x443;&#x458;  &#x443;
&#x43C;&#x43E;&#x458;&#x435;
 &#x441;&#x442;&#x438;&#x445;&#x43e;&#x432;&#x435;  &#x438;
&#x440;&#x438;&#x43c;&#x435;</red>
<red>Ka&#x434;  &#x442;&#x438;  &#x43a;a&#x436;&#x443;;,
&#x434;&#x440;a&#x433;a, &#x434;a
&#x442;&#x435;  &#x441;&#x438;&#x43b;&#x43d;&#x43e;
&#x432;o&#x43b;&#x438;&#x43c;;, </red>
<red>.....................................</red>
<red>.....................................</red>
</strofa>
</Pesma>
```

This document uses hexadecimal Unicode for Cyrillic letters. Here the problem of entering Unicode appears. Today, there are programs that can encode a document typed in Latin letters into Cyrillic Unicode (such a program can easily be created in any procedural programming language). Now the XML document display (using a browser) looks like this:

```
<?xml version="1.0" encoding="UTF-8" ?>
- <Pesma>
    <naslov>Ne veruj ...</naslov>
    <autor>Aleksa Šantić</autor>
    <datum>1905</datum>
  - <strofa>
      <red>Ne veruj u moje stihove i rime</red>
      <red>Kad ti kažu, draga, da te silno volim,</red>
      <red>.....................................</red>
      <red>.....................................</red>
    </strofa>
  </Pesma>
```

If the translation is performed using the Saxon processor, it is obtained in the form:

Service started.

Не веруј ...

Не веруј у моје стихове и риме
Кад ти кажу, драга, да те силно волим,
....
....

Алекса Шантић 1905

Service started.

If we make a change to the original text document by adding the command:

<?xml-stylesheet type="text/css" href="pesma.css" ?>,

then the display of this document, using a browser, looks like this:

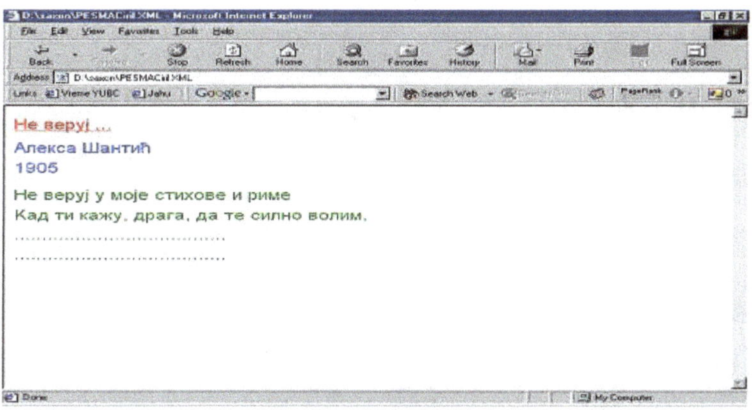

From the above examples it can be seen that the processing principles have not changed when working with the Cyrillic alphabet.

7. Conclusion

The previous section briefly described how some XML technologies (XHTML, XSLT, CSS) are used. From the examples given, it can be seen that the application of XML technologies requires knowledge of special languages and techniques. However, these technologies offer the possibility of transforming data in various ways. This is the main advantage of XML technology. Considering the above, we can conclude that the digitalization of data (the presentation of data in electronic form) should be based on XML and related technologies. This is a kind of guarantee that future generations will have easy access to this data. At the same time, the processing of such presented data will be maximally simplified.

References

[1] http://www.w3c.org

[2] http://www.w3.org

[3] http://www.w3.org/TR/1998/REC-xml-19980210+

[4] Hunter D.: Od početka ...XML, CET,Beograd 2001.

[5] Ladd E, O'Donnell J, Morgan M. and Watt A.H.: Using XHTML, XML and Java 2 , Que, 2000.

[6] http://users.iclway.co.uk/mhkay/saxon/

[7]http://www.unicode.org/charts/

6. USING SVG – XML FOR REPRESENTATION OF HISTORICAL GRAPHICAL DATA[4]

Abstract: Modern data representation requires XML-based approach. One of the ways to represent any kind of graphical data in electronic form is to use Scalable Vector Graphics (SVG). So, XML and SVG are ideal means for the digital representation of national heritage. Moreover, for the powerful using of SVG one should learn a very complex syntax and related XML applications. In this paper the advantages and drawbacks of SVG, in processing of national heritage, are specified. Some examples about processing frescos and manuscripts are presented.

1. Introduction

SVG is language for describing two-dimensional graphics in XML. In fact, it is a new technology aimed to support a workable cross-platform solution to Web imaging. A quite good description of SVG is stated in [1]: "Scalable Vector Graphics (SVG) is a new graphics file format and Web development language based on XML. SVG enables Web developers and designers to create dynamically generated, high-quality graphics from real time data with precise structural and visual control". SVG allows describing three types of graphic objects: vector graphic shapes (e.g., paths consisting of straight lines and curves), images and text. SVG-format is not proprietary. It is open standard built upon other open standards from the W3C and ECMA organizations. XML, CSS (Cascading Style Sheets), ECMAScript and SMIL (Synchronized Multimedia Integration Language) all contribute to the standard. SVG documents are described in XML so they can be easily generated and read by programs. SVG arose as a collaborative effort of some of the biggest experts in the computer world. As the result of their work the different recommendation documents appeared (see: [6], [7]). Nowadays we can find a lot of books related to SVG (see: [3], [4], [10]), but much more different articles on the Web (see: [2], [5], [9]). There are many applications that work with SVG data. According to these facts, we can conclude that SVG could be very useful for the digitalization of graphical, historical documents.

[4] The content of this chapter is taken from the work:
Tošić D., Filipović V. i Kratica J. : Using SVG – XML for representation of historical graphical data, Review of the National Center for Digitilization , 9 (2006), 39-45.

2. Some advantages and drawbacks of SVG

SVG is a XML-application. The grow of XML-technology predicts that it will be used much more in future. SVG is convenient for creation a new generation of Web applications based on:

- data-driven,
- interactive, and
- personalized graphics.

By this short characterizing we can see some good features of SVG. Moreover, there are much more reasons to accept SVG in processing of graphical data.

- SVG is based on XML – a general accepted language for description of data (emerging through the cooperative efforts of the World Wide Web Consortium (W3C) and its members) (see [8]).
- With SVG one can use existing skills (JavaScript language, Document Object Model (DOM), JSP, PHP, and ASP).
- SVG format is not proprietary. It is open standard built upon other open standards from the W3C and ECMA standards organizations.
- SVG is compatible text based and works seamlessly with current Web technologies like HTML, GIF, JPEG, PNG, SMIL, …
- Graphics created in SVG can be scaled without loss of quality across various platforms and devices.
- SVG is compatible with the languages used in wireless devices.
- …

As technical advantages of SVG (more details can be found in [5]), we can mention:

- Small file sizes
- Zoomable graphics
- Choice of large number of colors and fonts
- Scripting control for the interactive events and animation
- Bitmap-style filter effects for high-impact graphics
- …

Of course there are some drawbacks about using SVG (see [2]). We are mentioning some of them:

- contemporary browsers do not fully support SVG
- complex syntax and grammar of SVG
- lack of online SVG material in developing Web sites
- clumsy documentations
- close connection to the other XML applications
- ...

The lack of fully SVG support (from currently browsers) requires the use of a plug-in (see [1]). To plug in a SVG viewer one should download and install it. If all possibilities of SVG are not supported by the installed viewer, additional problems may appear. SVG is very rich language. It contains many built-in elements and large number of pre-defined constants. Because of that the syntax of SVG is not simple and related documentation is complex.

3. Structure of a SVG document

The structure of a SVG document is according to XML syntax. The following elements have to be included into SVG file:

1. **<?xml version="1.0" encoding="UTF-8"?>**

2. **<!DOCTYPE svg PUBLIC "-//W3C//DTD SVG 1.0//EN"**

   "http://www.w3.org/TR/2001/REC-SVG-20010904/DTD/svg10.dtd">

3. **<svg>**

4. **<!-- SVG content goes here -->**

5. **</svg>**

XML declaration <?xml version="1.0" encoding="UTF-8"> must be included in the beginning of SVG file. (This declaration could be a little different depending on encoding.) This declaration tells that the following content is a XML application. The next line is not obligated, but the part of this line where the standard is cited is required. We will include this part ("http://www.w3.org/2000/svg") in the third line. The second line is used to identify SVG as a standard set of rules. The <svg> tag indicates to the browser that this is a SVG document. The description of all SVG elements must be placed between the <svg> </svg> tags. Since SVG is a XML application, all tags must be closed. So </svg> is used to close the document.

In the next section we will used some of SVG elements, but without detailed description of these elements. The description could be found in [6] and [7] or in the books: [3], [10], …

4. How to process frescos and manuscripts by using SVG

In this part we put on some ideas about the processing of frescos and manuscripts by using the elements of SVG. In fact, we present some examples where the possibilities of SVG are used in showing and modifying of the digital images.

The frescos and manuscripts can be represented as the raster graphics, e.g. images based on pixel data (format: PNG, JPEG, GIF,…). SVG is vector-oriented and has limited possibility in dealing out with the raster images. However, some kinds of tasks can be done in digitization of these types of national heritage.

We can use <image> tag to present an image. In the following SVG file (named BeliAndjeo.svg) the image file BeliAndjeo.jpg is built-in.

```
<?xml version="1.0" encoding="UTF-8"?>

<svg xmlns="http://www.w3.org/2000/svg">

  <title>Beli Andjeo </title>

   <image x="10" y="10" width="400px" height="300px"

      xlink:href="BeliAndjeo.jpg">

   </image>

</svg>
```

IE (if SVG viewer is plug-in and the file BeliAndjeo.jpg is in the same folder as BeliAndjeo.svg) shows previous file in the following way:

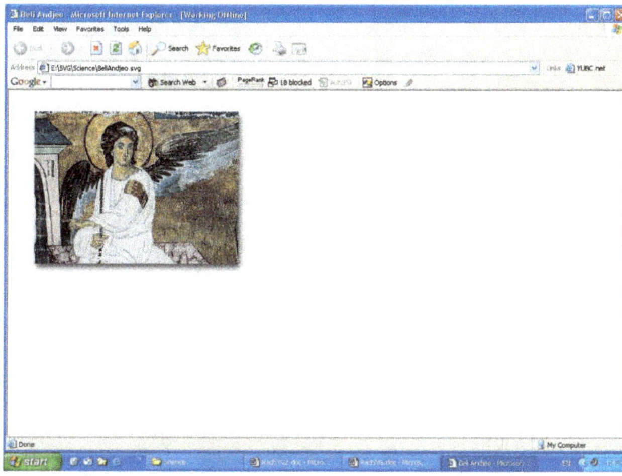

A SVG file may be embed into a HTML (XHTML) document by using <object> or <embed> tag. In the following example, <object> tag is used.

```
<html>
<head><title> White Angel</title></head>
<body>
<h2> WHITE ANGEL </h2>
<object data="BeliAndjeo.svg" type="image/svg+xml" width="400"
          height="300"></object>
<p>WHITE ANGEL - the fresco from Mileševa monastery</p>
<p>Mileševa monastery is foundation of king Vladislav (1234-1243).</br>
   Painting is from third decade of 13th century, before 1228.</p>
</body>
</html>
```

IE shows this file in the following manner:

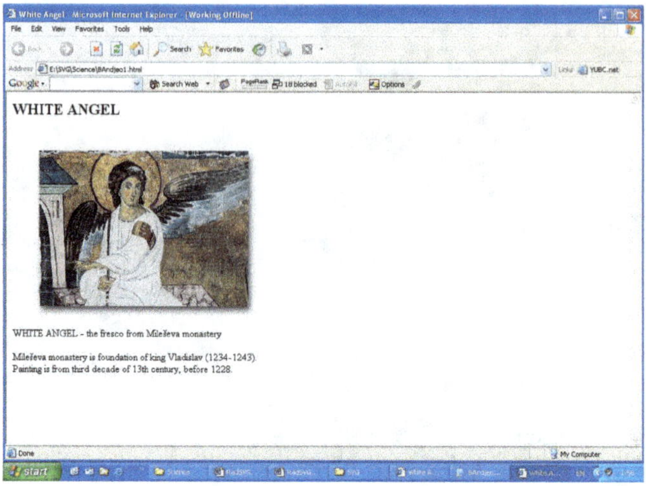

The images can be presented on different positions and in different sizes. The following SVG file contains the images from the manuscript “Miroslav's Gospel”:

```
<?xml version="1.0" encoding="UTF-8"?>

<svg xmlns="http://www.w3.org/2000/svg">

  <title> Miroslavovo jevandjelje </title>

    <image x="0" y="0" width="300px" height="400px"

        xlink:href="ME0.jpg"> </image>

    <image x="400" y="0" width="300px" height="400px"

        xlink:href="ME1.gif"> </image>

    <image x="0" y="410" width="100px" height="100px"

        xlink:href="ME0.jpg"> </image>

    <image x="150" y="410" width="100px" height="200px"

        xlink:href="ME1.gif"> </image>

    </image>

</svg>
```

If the files ME0.jpg and ME1.gif are in the same folder as previous file, IE will give:

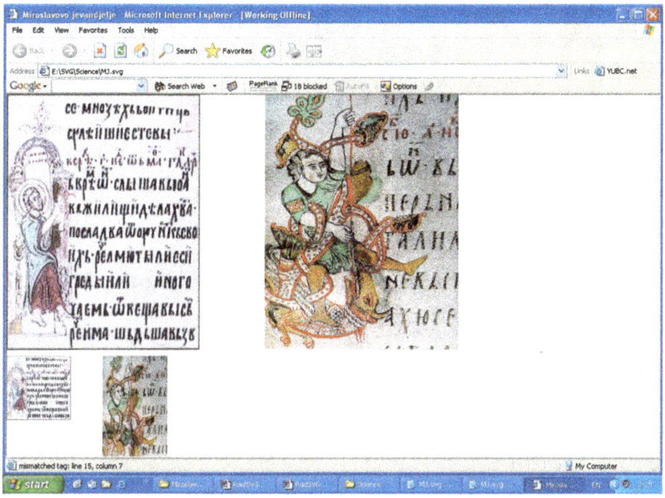

The original pictures could be changed by adding different figures and shapes. In the following example the red rectangle and blue circle are filled over the origin picture.

```
<?xml version="1.0" encoding="UTF-8"?>

<svg xmlns="http://www.w3.org/2000/svg">

  <title>Modifikovano Miroslavljevo jevandjelje</title>

    <image x="0" y="0" width="400px" height="500px"

        xlink:href="ME0.jpg"></image>

    <rect x="0" y="0" width="200" height="150" fill="red" />

    <circle cx="300" cy="300" r="50" fill="blue" />

</svg>
```

In this way we damage the original picture, because we get something like this:

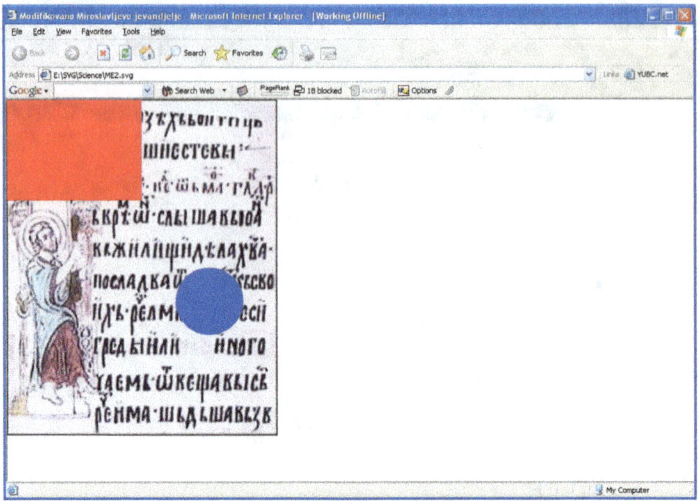

Moreover, the tags related to drawing and filling different shapes are very useful for the processing of original picture. We can delete, caver, color etc. the parts of an original picture. Using these techniques we can repair damages in the original picture or adapt the picture for some needs.

The text can be added to picture, too. SVG provides great possibilities in the presentation of text. In the next example, the rotated text is written over the manuscript:

```
<?xml version="1.0" encoding="UTF-8"?>

<svg xmlns="http://www.w3.org/2000/svg">

  <title>Modifikovano Miroslavljevo jevandjelje</title>

   <image x="0" y="0" width="400px" height="500px"

      xlink:href="ME0.jpg"></image>

      <g transform="rotate(20)">

        <text x="100" y="100" font-size="36"

           font-family="sans-serif" fill="red" >

           Text overe the manuscript!

        </text>
```

```
        </g>
    </svg>
```

Te result of this processing is following:

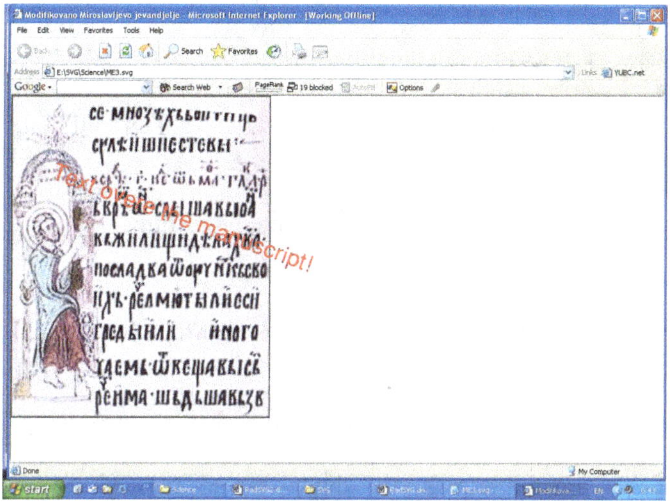

These examples show only some of SVG possibilities in processing national heritage represented by images. Of course, we can do much more, but through these examples we demonstrate some simple opportunities of SVG.

5. Conclusion

XML technology is a good choose for the digitization of national heritage. The presence of large number of images in our cultural heritage needs adequate processing of 2Dgraphics. So, the natural choice is the XML graphical application, i.e. SVG. By using XML markup, we can create and implement graphic images, animations, and interactive opportunities. We can expect that SVG will become a standard language (technology) for the processing of graphical cultural heritage.

References

[1] Adobe on SVG http://www.adobe.com/svg

[2] Duce D: Scalable Vector Graphics (SVG): Vector Graphics for the Web, http://www.ariadne.ac.uk/issue28/graphics, 2001.

[3] Eisenberg D. J: SVG Essentials, Oreilly, 2002.

[4] Holzner S: Sams Teach Yourself XML in 21 Days, Third Edition, Sams Publishing, 2003.

[5] Holzschlag M.E: Scalable Vector Graphics, http://www.webtechniques.com/ archives/2001/04/desi/, 2001.

[6] Scalable Vector Graphics (SVG), Specification 1.1, http://www.w3.org/ TR/SVG11/

[7] Scalable Vector Graphics (SVG) 1.2, http://www.w3.org/TR/SVG12/

[8] Tošić D: XML-tehnologije i digitalizacija, Pregled nacionalnog centra za digitalizaciju, 3, pp. 1-12, 2003.

[9] Traversa E. Scalable Vector Graphics: The Art is in the Code, http://wwwwebrefrence.com/authoring/languages/svg , 2001.

[10] Watt A., Chris Lilley C. et. al: SVG Unleashed, Sams Publis

7.
POTENTIAL ROLE OF SMIL IN DIGITALIZATION OF NATIONAL HERITAGE[5]

Abstract. XML technologies provide that digitalization of national heritage relies on widely accepted standards. Beside the XML standardized way of text and picture digitalization, there is a similar way for multimedia digitalization. Special XML language, called SMIL (Synchronized Multimedia Integration Language) is used for the multimedia digitalization. This language is very convenient for the digitalization of national heritage like the custom, national dresses, popular national music etc. The SMIL capabilities in digitalization (its good and bad sides) are described shortly in this paper. Several specific examples, demonstrating SMIL characteristics and possible using in digitalization of multimedia heritage, are presented.

1. Introduction

SMIL is a language for synchronized multimedia integration – it serves for the describing of multimedia. Like XHTML, SVG etc, SMIL is created according to the XML rules. The languages like SMIL are often called XML applications (see [8] and [9]). SMIL is made by W3C and the work on its specification started in 1998. Until now the versions SMIL 1.0, SMIL 2.1 and WD-SMIL 3 are created (see [3] and [4]). All SMIL versions are fully based on XML. Version SMIL 1.0 provides all classical video and audio elements (like TV, movi, ...). The version SMIL 2.1 is compatible with SMIL 1.0, but it has additional capabilities: it provides modularity and extends some functionality. So SMIL 2.1 is a superset of previous version. WD-SMIL 3 is proposed in December 2006 and it is draft version. This version is superset related to SMIL 2.1.

What are benefits in the using SMIL instead of classical audio and video documents? The multimedia contents expressed by SMIL can be easily manipulated with, easily presented on the Web, easily recorded etc. W3C recommendations are widely accepted and it is really to expect that SMIL becomes global official standard for multimedia documents in the future. One can conclude that, in this moment, SMIL is the best language for the digitalization of multimedia documents in national heritage. This

---

[5] The content of this chapter is taken from the work:
Tošić D., Filipović V, Tuba M. And Kratica J.: Potential Role of SMIL in Digitalization of National Heritage, Review of the National Center for Digitilization, 10 (2007), 33-39.

practically means that SMIL is especially convenient whenever pictures and sounds are combined. For instance, SMIL is convenient for representation of folk dance, for registering some special events (weddings), national customs, etc.

2. Characteristics of SMIL

SMIL is a language used for the creation of multimedia documets and their presentations. Those presentations define what will be shown, where will be shown, when will be shown and how long it will last. In the other words, SMIL presentations have defined timescale. One of the biggest SMIL presentations advantage is the fact that those presentations can easily be found on Internet. (Increasing the numer of documents at Internet bears a new problem: how to find the right document. All XML based documents, peincipally, could be easier found then the others.)

As we already said, a SMIL-document is, in same time, XML based document, which begins with tag <smil> and end with closing tag </smil>. Similar to plain HTML, there are child tags <head> and <body> (and their closing counterparts) within <smil> tag. The role of these tags is similar to the corresponding tags in HTML. The main differences in corresponding to HTML are:

- the SMIL tags have to be written in lower case (SMIL is case-sensitive).
- SMIL is XML-based. Tags have to be ended.

Some characteristics of SMIL and some examples are described in [1], [2], [6] and [7]. The complete description of different SMIL-versions could be found on the sites [3], [4] and [5].

The skeleton of a correct SMIL document can be described in the following way:

```
<smil>

 <head>

 <meta name="Faculty of Mathematics" content="Teaching" />

 <layout>

  <!— positioning tags -->

 </layout>

 </head>
```

```
<body>
 <!— content tags, time tags, synchronization tags -->
</body>
</smil>
```

As the other Web-technologies, SMIL has some weaknesses. Major SMIL weaknesses are pointed out in [1]:

- confusion in terminology and
- lack of business and art support.

Today, there are a large number of software products supporting multimedia. Each software vendor forces its terminology, and that area is not stabilized yet. This weakness will be probably less important when the Web-technology becomes stable.

SMIL also has a weakness common to whole XML based documents – it is complexity of XML-technology. XML applications are truly powerful when they are combined and when they relied on each other. However, that combining requires many efforts: studing different XML applications, using a loto of software tools, …

Sometimes "technical problems" arise because exist different SMIL versions and some SMIL player vendors don't support SMIL 2.0 and WD-SMIL 3 . However, in close future this "technical problems" will probably be overridden.

3. What can we do with SMIL?

At the original site of W3C related to SMIL (see [4]), we find the short description: "SMIL is typically used for "rich media"/multimedia presentations which integrate streaming audio and video with images, text or any other media type".

According to [6], by using SMIL, we can:

- position media elements wherever we want on the screen,
- synchronize those elements,
- display media following user-preferences, language, bit-rate, etc

The positions of media elements can be relative or absolute. To insert the media within a presentation we have to specify the region (the right place into main window) where it will be displayed. One media element can be positioned over the other by adding zindex attribute to <region>. Also, each media element may be adapted to its container by using the "fit" attribute. If the media element is bigger than its region, the area can be scrolled by setting the fit attribute to "scroll". Working with timeline provides synchronization of media elements by using <par> and <seq> tags.

4. Using of SMIL

SMIL document is in a text format, saved within file with extension SMIL. So, to write a SMIL-application, we can use a usual text-editor like Notepad from Windows. Moreover, there are special editors (for example, VM) adapting to the SMIL-syntax and very convenient for writing SMIL-documents.

The adequate software tool (also known as player or multimedia browser) is required to "show" a specific SMIL document. There are many players on the market (see [1], [5] and [6]). One of the most popular for Windows systems is RealOne Player (produced by RealNetworks).

To demonstrate how to use SMIL, we will consider a simple example.

Suppose that the following SMIL-document is in the file **Prvi.smil**:

```
<smil>
 <head>
  <layout>
   <root-layout width="600" height="600" background-color="green" />
  </layout>
 </head>
 <body>
   <text src="text.txt" />
 </body>
</smil>
```

One can notice that within SMIL document exists reference to file **text.txt** (in <text> tag). Let the file **text.txt** contains:

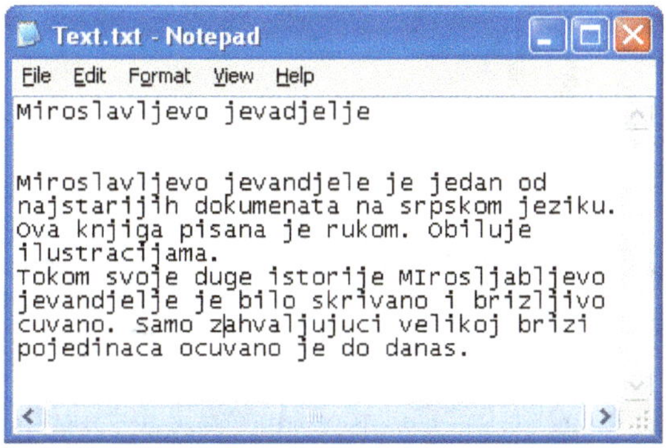

Browsing folder containing the file **Prvi.smil** will show icon representation of thatSMIL file. That icon looks like:

The activation of this icon (by click or double-click, depending on Windows settings) will activate RealPlayer application, and show SMIL document:

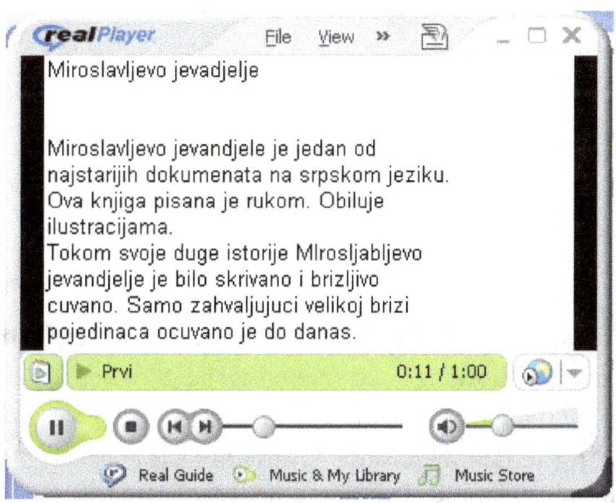

5. Examples related to digitalization of cultural heritage

The following examples demonstrate only small subset of SMIL capabilities. The detail presentation of SMIL constructions requires much more space. Several interesting examples for using SMIL can be found in [1] and [7].

Example 1. Create a SMIL presentation that simultaneously shows both picture and text. Picture is in the file **Miroslav.jpg**, and text is in the file **Text.txt**.

```
<smil>
 <head>
  <layout>
   <root-layout width="500" height="500" background-color="white" />
   <region id="Reg1" left="75" top="50" width="300" height="300" />
   <region id="Reg2" left="150" top="300" width="300" height="180" />
  </layout>
 </head>
 <body>
  <par>
   <img src="Miroslav.jpg" alt="This is a picture" region="Reg1" dur="20s" />
   <text src="Text.txt" region="Reg2" />
  </par>
 </body>
</smil>
```

In the previous example, the files with picture and text are within <body> tag. The duration of picture showing is 20 seconds. The tag <head> contains size of presentation window, size and position of window that contains text and size and position of picture window. All presentation settings are within <layout> tag, that is inside <head> tag. On the beginning the presented contains is follow:

After 20 seconds the picture will disappear and only text will stay.

Example 2. Modify previous example presenting the picture and text sequentially. First the picture should be shown for 10 seconds and after that the text should be shown for 15 seconds.

```
<smil>
 <head>
  <layout>
   <root-layout width="500" height="500" background-color="red" />
   <region id="Reg1"  left=100 top=100  width="300" height="300"  fit="fill" />
  </layout>
 </head>
 <body>
  <seq>
   <img src="Miroslav.jpg" alt="This is pictur" region="Reg1" dur="10s" />
```

<text src="Text.txt" region="Reg1" dur="10s" />

</seq>

</body>

</smil>

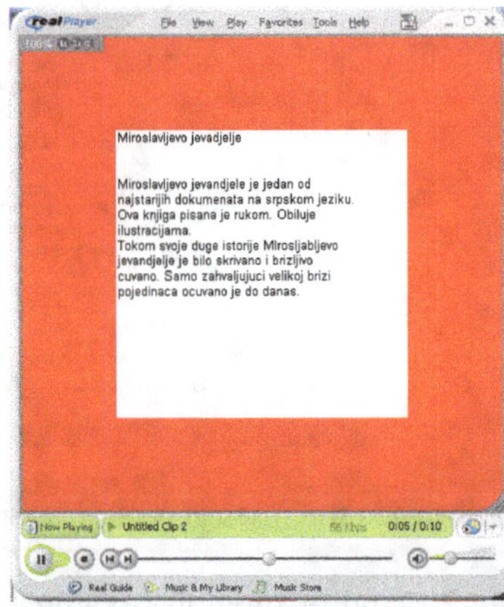

The background color in this example is red. Region for text and picture showing is positioned almost in the centre of main window. The fit attribute is used and both, picture and text are fitted into region.

Example 3. Create SMIL presentation that firstly shows a short movie about Belgrade. After 10 seconds in the same region should be shown textual explanation and that explanation should last for 5 seconds. In the background of movi and text, one should listen to soft music represented by the file >

<layout>

<root-layout width="500" height="500" background-color="yellow" />

<region id="Reg1" width="600" height="500" fit="fill" />

</layout>

</head>

<body>

```
  <seq>
    <par>
      <audio src="Greetings.wma"/>
      <img src="Bekgrade.avi" region="Reg1" dur="10s"/>
    </par>
    <par>
     <audio src=" Greetings.wma"/>
     <text src="Text1.txt" region="Reg1" dur="5s"/>
    </par>
  </seq>
</body>
</smil>
```

We can not show here the screen with movie, neither listen to music. So we will omit realPlayer presentation of this SMIL document.

6. Conclusion

Previous examples show that SMIL can be used easily. SMIL is similar to HTML, so SMIL constructions can be easily understood by HTML proficient reader. Of course, in order to create more complex document, the authors have to know syntax and effects of various SMIL tags. The main advantage of SMIL (comparing to the other multimedia techniques) is standardized XML-like document format. Therefore, browsing and working with SMIL documents on Internet is very easy. W3C has large influence on Internet and we can expect that SMIL will be accepted as universal XML application and standard multimedia document format.

References

[1] Arciniegas A F, .A Realist's SMIL Manifesto, http://www.xml.com/pub/a/2002/05/29/smil.html, 2002.

[2] Bouthillier L. Synchronized Multimedia On The Web - A New W3C Format Is All Smiles, http://www.webtechniques.com/archives/1998/09/bouthillier , 1998.

[3] http://www.w3.org/TR/SMIL2/ , 2005.

[4] http://www.w3.org/TR/2006/WD-SMIL3-20061220/

[5] http://en.wikipedia.org/wiki/Synchronized_Multimedia_Integration_Language

[6] http://www.helio.org/products/smil/tutorial, 1999.

[7] Zeldman J. SMIL When You Play That, http://www.aliestapart.com/articles/smil/, 1999.

[8] Tošić D.: "XML-tehnologije i digitalizacija", Pregled nacionalnog centra za digitalizaciju, 3 (2003), 1-12.

[9] Tošić D., Filipović V. and Kratica J.: Using SVG – XML for representation of historical graphical data, Review of the National Center for Digitilization 9 (2006), 39-45.

8.
MATHML – APPLICATION OF XML

Mathematical Markup Language (MathML) is an application of XML for describing mathematical notation, ie. representing mathematical expressions and formulas. What is the role of MathML in the digitalization process? Since it is based on XML, MathML has an important role in the digitalization process, as well as XML. However, the field of application of this language is considerably narrow. Mathematics and its symbolism have been developed for centuries. Therefore, it is not easy to create a descriptive language that would be easy to use and satisfy all other requirements that XML applications fulfill. The records of individual mathematical expressions are often more complicated than in other descriptive languages intended for the recording of mathematical expressions and formulas. MathML is not a programming language and cannot be used to calculate the value of expressions or solve equations, but it enables the display of expressions, matrices, partial differential equations, integral equations, etc. To introduce MathML, we will describe several tags and give examples of where and how these tags are used. However, this is not a MathML tutorial. For a more detailed introduction to MathML, see [1] and [2].

The **math element** is the root of all MathML expressions. Therefore, it needs to be declared as well as other XML elements. This is done in the following way:

```
<math xmlns=http://www.w3.org/1998/Math/MathML
            display = "inline" >
  <mrow>...</mrow>
</math>
```

MathML expressions can be incorporated into an XML or HTML document. XML is closely related to HTML and assumes a very similar, but not identical syntax. For example, in XML one cannot omit end tags, but it is possible in HTML.

MathML characterizes a number of XML tags which can be used into math elements. Each element, into Math element, can take several attributes. Some basic tags are:

mrow — displays its subelements in a horizontal row

mi — represents an identifier such as the name of a function or variable

mo — represents an operator or delimiter

mn — represents a number

The following examples demonstrate the use of previously described tags, as well as some more frequently used in mathematical expressions and formulas ([3], [4]).

Example 1. Expression:

p=a*b-2

is written, using MathML, in the following way:

```
<math>
 <mrow>
  <mrow>
   <mi>p</mi>
   <mo>=</mo>
   <mi>a</mi>
   <mo>*</mo>
   <mi>b</mi>
   <mo>-</mo>
   <mn>2</mn>
  </mrow>
</math>
```

Example 2. Here we demonstrate the use of the mfrac tag when writing the fraction:

$$\frac{x}{10}$$

```
<math xmlns=http://www.w3.org/1998/Math/MathML
                              display="inline">
<mfrac>
 <mrow>
  <mi>x</mi>
 </mrow>
 <mn>10</mn>
</mfrac>
</math>
```

Example 3. Expression

$$(a-1)^{3x+5}$$

contains new tag msup and could be written by MathML in the following way:

```
<math xmlns="http://www.w3.org/1998/Math/MathML"
                                   display="inline">
  <msup>
     <mrow>
    <mo>(</mo>
    <mi>a</mi>
     <mo>-</mo>
     <mn>1</mn>
     <mo>)</mo>
```

```
        </mrow>
   <mrow>
     <mn>3</mn>
     <mi>x</mi>
     <mo>+</mo>
     <mn>5</mn>
   </mrow>
  </msup>
</math>
```

Example 4. Expression:

$$\sqrt[5]{x+y}$$

is presented by MathML (with new tag **mroot**) in the following way:

```
<math xmlns="http://www.w3.org/1998/Math/MathML"
                              display="inline">
  <mrow>
   <mroot>
     <mrow>
      <mi>x</mi>
      <mo>+</mo>
      <mi>y</mi>
     </mrow>
     <mn>5</mn>
```

```
    </mroot>

</mrow>

</math>
```

Example 5.

By using HTML and MathML, we write an abstract for a scientific paper that serves to solve an integral equation. The text is written in HTML, and the integral equation is written using MathML. Invoking MathML expressions from HTML is demonstrated.

```
<html>

<center>

<h2><center>DISCRETIZATION AND NUMERICAL SOLUTION OF
NONLINEAR INTEGRAL EQUATIONS </h2>

<h4>Dušan TOŠIĆ and Nikola PERIN </h4>

<div  align=left><p><b>Abstract.</b> The problem of finding a numerical solution
for the nonlinear integral equation: </p></div>

<!- -  Here we begin writing the integral equation by using MathML  -->

<math xmlns="http://www.w3.org/1998/Math/MathML"

                                                  display="inline">

 <mrow>

   <mi>y</mi><mo>(</mo><mi>x</mi>

   <mo>)</mo> <mo>-</mo>

    <mrow>

        <msubsup>

          <mo>&int;</mo>

             <mi>a</mi><mi>x</mi>
```

```
        </msubsup>
     <mrow>
        <mi>K</mi><mo>[</mo>
        <mi>x</mi><mo>,</mo>
        <mi>s</mi><mo>,</mo>
        <mi>y</mi> <mo>(</mo>
        <mi>s</mi><mo>)</mo>
        <mo>]</mo>
     <mrow>
       <mi>d</mi>
       <mi>s</mi>
     </mrow>
    </mrow>
     <mrow>
      <mo>=</mo><mi>f</mi><mo>     (</mo><mi>x</mi><mo>)</mo>
     </mrow>
<center>
</math>
<div  align=justify>
is considered. Two methods for the discretization are proposed. The first method is based on the numerical integration and interpolation. In the second method, the Euler-McLaurin  formula and numerical derivation are used. </div>
</html>
```

By entering this content into the file m3.html and starting this file through the Google Chrome browser, the following view is obtained.

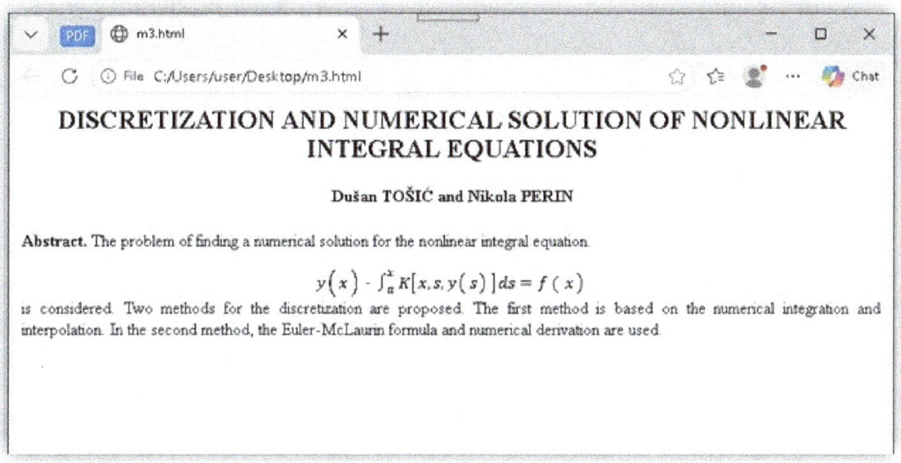

DISCRETIZATION AND NUMERICAL SOLUTION OF NONLINEAR INTEGRAL EQUATIONS

Dušan TOŠIĆ and Nikola PERIN

Abstract. The problem of finding a numerical solution for the nonlinear integral equation

$$y(x) - \int_a^x K[x, s, y(s)]\,ds = f(x)$$

is considered. Two methods for the discretization are proposed. The first method is based on the numerical integration and interpolation. In the second method, the Euler-McLaurin formula and numerical derivation are used.

Conclusion

MathML enables the recording of mathematical content in accordance with XML. As XML is of great importance for digitalization in general, MathML is also important for digitalization in mathematics. Instead of various symbols for: integrals, sums, roots, ... we can now write all this using text with alfanumeric signs. Unlike XML, tags in MathML are predefined. There are several dozen of them and only a few of them are used here to give some insight into the possibilities of MathML. As MathML was created from XML, other XML applications are created and used in a similar way.

References

[1] https://www.w3.org/Math/whatIsMathML.html

[2] https://www.w3.org/TR/mathml4/

[3] Hussein Shafie: MathML Presentation Markup for the Impatient, https://www.xmlmind.com/tutorials/MathML/, 2025.

[4] Creating equations with MathML, https://www.drillster.com › info, 2026.

9.
RELATED WORKS

The following works (in which D. Tošić is a co-author) are related to XML, but are not used in this book:

[1] Quarsma P., Janičić P., Tomašević J., V.-Janičić M. and Tošić D.: XML –Based Format for Description of Geometrical Constructions and Proofs, in Comunicating Mathematics in the Digital Era, (ed. Borwein J. M., Rocha E.M. and Rodrigues J. F.) A. K. Peters, Ltd. pp. 183-197, 2008.

[2] Filipović, V., Zagarčanin M., Tošić D. and Stanišić S.: "Digitalization in the Bar county museum – pilot project", Review of the National Cenatar for Digitalization, Issue 23, pp. 57-66, 2013.

[3] Emhimed Salem Alatrish, Dušan Tošić and Nikola Milenković: "Building ontologies for different natural languages", Computer Science and Information Systems, Vol. 11, No. 2, 623–644, 2014.

[4] Šandrih, Branislava; Tošić, Dušan; and Filipović, Vladimir: Towards Efficient and UnifiedXML/JSON Conversion - A New Conversion, Method. Transactions on Internet Research (TIR), 13(1):58–64, January 2017.

www.ingramcontent.com/pod-product-compliance
Lightning Source LLC
LaVergne TN
LVHW022305200926
848481LV00004B/1227

* 9 7 9 8 8 9 9 6 6 4 7 2 4 *